STOLEN BABIES OF SPAIN: THE BOOK

Truth. Justice. Reconciliation.

Greg Rabidoux

Mara Lencina

Enrique Vila Torres

First Edition: March 2020
Library of Congress Control Number: 2020903820
ISBN 978-1-7352716-0-6 Hardcover
ISBN 978-0-578-65418-8 Paperback

Front and back cover design by Greg Rabidoux and Valentin Lencina-Rabidoux

Printed in USA by ValMar Books
(a division of ValMar Productions, Inc.)
Myrtle Beach, South Carolina
www.stolenbabiesofspain.com
www.facebook.com/stolenbabiesofspain
www.imdb.com/title/tt11219178/

This book is dedicated to all the stolen baby victims of Spain, and around the globe, their families, and loved ones, who, despite incredible odds and official indifference and opposition, continue to search for truth, justice, and reconciliation. May you all be blessed in your search and find peace of mind at the end of your journey.

Este libro está dedicado a todas las víctimas de bebés robados de España y de todo el mundo, a sus familias y seres queridos, quienes, a pesar de las bajas probabilidades y la indiferencia y oposición oficiales, continúan buscando la verdad, la justicia, y la reconciliación. Que todos sean bendecidos en su búsqueda y encuentren paz y tranquilidad al final del arduo trayecto.

Praise for Stolen Babies of Spain: The Book

"Han sucedido muchas cosas desde que comencé mi viaje para descubrir mis verdaderos orígenes y Mara y Greg estuvieron allí en los momentos cruciales justo antes, durante y después del juicio del Dr. Vela en el 2018. Estoy orgullosa de ser parte de su documental y este libro. Espero que a medida que más personas en todo el mundo vean su película y lean este libro, comprendan no solo lo que sucedió en España, sino que ayuden a difundir los hechos para que las víctimas puedan conseguir de una vez por todas la verdad, la reconciliación y la justicia que buscan.

Tan sorprendentes, tristes e increíbles como son las historias que aparecen en este libro, recuerde que podría haberle sucedido a cualquiera. Por favor, comparta este libro con alguien al que ama."

"So much has happened since when I began my own journey to find out my true origins and Mara and Greg were there at the crucial moments right before, during and after the trial of Dr. Vela in 2018. I am proud to be a part of their documentary film and this book. I hope as more people around the world watch their film and read this book they will come to understand not only what took place in Spain but help spread the word so that victims can once and for all gain the truth, reconciliation and justice they seek.

As stunning and sad and amazing as the stories inside this book are, please remember that it could have happened to anyone. Please share this book with someone you love."

Inés Madrigal
Victim and President of Murcia's Stolen Babies Association

"Como presidenta de la Asociación de Bebés Robados de Alicante, este libro es de vital importancia para ayudar a llevar al público las historias de víctimas de todas partes. Los casos compartidos en Stolen Babies of Spain: The Documentary y aquí, en forma escrita, pueden ser sorprendentes, ¡pero la gente necesita saber la verdad!"

"As the president of the Association of Stolen Babies of Alicante, this book is vitally important to help get the stories of victims everywhere to the public. The cases shared in *Stolen Babies of Spain: The Documentary* and here, in written form, may be stunning but people need to know the truth!"

María José Picó
Victim and President of Alicante's Stolen Babies Association

"Primero le conté mi historia a Mara en una concentración de víctimas de robos de bebés en Valencia en el 2018. Estaba contenta y agradecida por la oportunidad de contar mi historia, ahora me siento orgullosa y espero que mi experiencia pueda ayudar de alguna manera a otros a descubrir su propia verdad y obtener la justicia que todos buscamos."

"I first told my story to Mara at a Stolen Baby victims rally in Valencia in 2018. I was proud then and grateful for the opportunity, and I am proud now and hope my experience may hopefully somehow help others discover their own truth and to get the justice we all seek."

Paqui Bria
Victim

"Cuando Greg, Mara y su equipo llegaron a Cádiz para filmar dos exhumaciones y me pidieron que compartiera la búsqueda de mi hermana, supe que querían descubrir la pura verdad y ayudarnos a todas las víctimas. Este libro es otro paso en ese importante camino hacia la verdad."

"When Greg and Mara and their film crew came to Cadiz to film two exhumations and they asked me to share my own search for my sister, I knew they wanted to find out the real truth and help all us victims. This book is another step in that important journey."

Chary Herrera
Victim and President of Cadiz's Stolen Babies Association

"Este libro, junto con la película del mismo título, son valiosos medios para ayudar y fortalecer a las víctimas de todo el mundo, dar visibilidad a la Causa y a la vez, una viva contribución de la lucha para reivindicar y exigir justicia. En la película, agito con fuerza unos cencerros (o campanas) al paso de la multitud y así, despertar sus mentes y su atención para que se detengan ante nuestros carteles de búsquedas. Es realmente gratificante y emocionante ver la respuesta solidaria de la gente que se sensibiliza y firma nuestras peticiones inherentes a la defensa de los valores y la dignidad humana. Sin duda, este libro que narra nuestra lucha por la verdad es el broche final de esta gran obra que te llega al corazón."

"This book, together with the film of the same title, are a valuable means to help and strengthen the victims around the world, to give visibility to the Cause and at the same time, a living contribution of the struggle to claim and demand justice. In the movie, I shake some cowbells (or bells) as the crowds pass and so, awaken their minds and attention to stop before our search posters. It is really gratifying and exciting to see the unified response of the people who are sensitized and who sign our requests inherent in the defense of values and human dignity. Undoubtedly, this book that tells our fight for the truth, is the final touch of this great work that reaches your heart."

Antonio Iniesta
Victim

"Aunque no pude estar en la película, estoy orgullosa de ser parte de este libro. Compartir mi historia, junto con tantos otros que están buscando y con un perfil aquí, nos da esperanza y todos estamos agradecidos por cada persona que lee sobre nuestra lucha."
"I am proud to be part of this book. Sharing my story, along with so many others who are searching and are profiled here, gives us hope and we are all grateful for anyone and everyone who reads about our struggles."

Eva Páramos
Victim

"Mara, Greg y Valentín vinieron a nuestra casa y nos filmaron a mi madre y a mí compartiendo la historia de nuestra búsqueda, de su hija y mi hermana. Nos complace que este libro proporcione otra forma de dar visibilidad a las víctimas."
"Mara, Greg and Valentin came to our home and filmed us as my mother, and I shared our story of our search for her daughter and my sister. We are pleased that this book provides another way to give visibility to the victims."

Mari Feli Navalón
Victim

Table of Contents

Preface

It began, for us at least, with a phone call and a question. Would your mother be willing to talk to Mara, who was researching stories of stolen babies in Spain as part of her dissertation for a university in America?

"I don't know," her daughter replied, "she really doesn't like to talk about what happened. It still hurts a lot for her to even think about it. I suppose there's no harm in asking though."

Later that summer and then again for our cameras in the summer of 2018, her mother, Paquita, did open-up about what happened. And we are forever grateful to her and all the wonderful mothers, fathers, grandparents, daughters and sons, sisters and brothers, aunts and uncles who have since talked with us and shared their own personal stories of separation, struggle and betrayal. Many chose to voluntarily do so for the camera, while many more chose to be interviewed for this book only. Still, some victims shared their own tale of hardship with us but only on the condition we not "out" them for fear of retaliation by those in power, by those who they are convinced still want to keep the truth dead and buried. We have done our best to honor all such requests.

We have conducted more than 300 interviews over the past 5 years. Known victims and those with cases new to us continued to contact us nearly every week right up to the publication of this book to share their stories. Upon reflection, we continue to be struck by the courage, persistence and the sheer humanity of all victims and their loved ones. We are still in awe of what they have gone through and the pain, frustration and yes, hope, they still feel as they continue to search for truth, justice and reconciliation in a system determined to fight them every step of the way.

1

As we traveled across Spain filming *Stolen Babies of Spain: The Documentary*, we met victims at public gatherings like rallies, protests, assemblies, marches, sporting events, cafes, and in church gatherings, both solemn and happy. We also met with several in more private settings where victims invited us in and made us feel welcome. Despite the pain they carried with them we were always warmly embraced. Each victim went out of their way to make us feel part of their family as they opened-up their hearts, homes and family photo-albums to us.

Though many have thanked us for helping tell their story to the world it is we, who are forever grateful.

We are indeed honored and humbled by the trust and faith they have placed in us and our work.

What follows in the coming chapters is our good faith effort to share their stories, their struggles and their dreams with each of you, the readers. In the end, we hope that a more informed and aware world may somehow help each to find the truth, justice and reconciliation they seek. And that ultimately, they can each become whole once again.

Across Spain to the west and east, north and south, no region or province or city or town or village seems immune from this tragedy. No family seems completely unaffected by the stealing of babies that has now gone on for over six decades.

In fact, no part of Spain has been left untouched or untainted by these crimes. We continue to be stunned by how eerily similar the stories of deception, fraud and theft of loved ones are by those we have interviewed. And it made no difference who we spoke with nor where they lived in Spain. The stories told and the tears shed were both real and all too familiar.

They are stories brimming with very human accounts of trust being betrayed by doctors, nurses, priests and politicians. Of cases being closed by prosecutors despite overwhelming evidence to the contrary. Of an endless search that leads only to more lies, more deception and more frustration.

Reliable estimates have conservatively placed the number of stolen baby victims at over 300,000. But many believe this number is even higher. And the number grows exponentially in terms of the families and friends these thefts have and continue to affect, to harm and to cause emotional pain.

These are crimes without any seeming end to their moral depravity nor their capacity to cause pain and suffering across all ages, all genders, all generations.

In the coming chapters you will also get to know up close and personal several of the victims on a level never before shared with readers. These are their stories in their own words. And we are grateful for their trust and willingness to open up to us and now you, about their struggle. Many have been honest about the fear they feel in coming forward. They fear retaliation for simply telling the world the truth-that their own government, their church, their caregivers lied to them, covered-up the truth and continue to suppress evidence and block their path to justice. They fear they will lose their jobs, their livelihoods, maybe even their own lives as they pursue the road to discovery.

But still, they come forward.

"What else can they take?" asks one victim, "that they have not already taken?"

We also greatly appreciate the contributions of Enrique Vila to this book. An author, lawyer and victim himself, he shares for the first time ever, details previously undisclosed of several of his cases he has handled on behalf of stolen baby victims like himself, both in Spain and the USA. For nearly three decades Mr. Vila has been bringing forth cases on behalf of stolen baby victims. In 2011 he and a colleague filed a class action suit citing 261 such cases before the Spanish Court. The first such filing of its kind in Spain's history.

Today, he continues to advocate on behalf of victims globally. He recently had a personal meeting with Pope Francis to persuade him to open Catholic Church adoption records in Spain and brought the fight before the United Nations Committee on the Rights of the Child, also the first such case of its kind.

You'll learn more about his story and some of his more dramatic stolen baby cases soon.

But right now, let's turn the page and in the *Prologue,* we'll introduce you to some very courageous people whose determination to find out the truth against all odds make them anything but victims.

Prologue

The Mafia.

That's the word that victims use to describe the criminal network that stole their babies at birth.

Not the mafia which many, especially in America think of when they hear this word. No, the Spanish mafia is not like the one depicted and glamourized as only Hollywood can do in blockbuster films like *The Godfather*. (1)

At least the mafia in those films paid lip service to supposedly cherished institutions of family, faith and taking care of your "own."

In Spain, this mafia or criminal network tore apart families, exploited the blind faith of followers to betray them and preyed upon members of their own society. All the while being aided and abetted by the Catholic Church. The church was eager to regain its own power and relevance which had greatly receded under the progressive Second Republic (1931-1939) prior to the Spanish Civil War. And if this meant sacrificing some of its own flock on the altar of organized corruption then so be it. (2)

As Sister María of the Santa Cristina clinic in Madrid remarked, "We did nothing wrong. We answered to a higher calling." (3)

The mafia of Hollywood? In Spain, fact was even more cruel and heartless than fiction.

But why steal babies? Why did this mafia network conspire and commit itself to the stealing and selling of its own babies?

As we'll learn more in *Chapter 1*, initially, it was for political and ideological reasons. Taking babies was a way to punish and destroy survivors suspected of being sympathetic to the vanquished Spanish Republicans who fought against Franco's

Nationalist forces during the Spanish Civil War. Inspired by Nazi eugenics and led by psychiatrists like Antonio Vallejo-Nágera, who relied heavily on pseudo-science to justify these destructive policies, the goal was always the same-eradicate and eliminate any surviving "red gene" or socialist DNA strand disloyal to Franco in the new, emerging Spanish society. The belief was that any mentally deficient socialist tendencies would then eventually die off, and never return.

And if it took "redistributing" thousands of Spanish babies from their "morally deficient" and "ideologically bankrupt" biological parents to do what was best for Spain then so be it. As Vallejo-Nágera often told his fellow Spaniards, "it was after all, God's will on earth." (4)

Gradually though, the sinister genetic and political motives behind these horrific crimes morphed into what crimes almost always seem to be about. Greed. An insatiable lust for profit. Baby stealing became a boom business in a newly emerging, post-war Spain. And those in the mafia network became fat, rich and happy. All at the expense of an unknowing, trusting and painfully obedient society.

Spaniards had been conditioned to trust and obey the uniform and those who wore it of their military and their church. They did as they were told, and it cost them. Dearly.

Like a cancer, this criminal mafia cell spread fast. With no clearly defined beginning or end it continued to grow all the while defying capture and evading criminal conviction.

To this day it still does.

This is a mafia which implicates doctors and nurses, revered priests and nuns, respected government leaders and bureaucrats. Its tentacles connects everyone from gravediggers, DNA laboratory technicians, "baby cabbies" or taxi-cab drivers paid to illegally transport stolen babies in-between so-called "stolen baby

6

corridors" in Spain to high-profile cabinet-level officials all the way to Rome and the Pope perched on his throne in the Vatican. Victims point an accusing finger over the last several decades at these individuals and more as all being part of and playing a role in this criminal network conceived for the purpose of stealing and selling their babies in Spain and beyond its borders for profit. Either they took an active part or knew about the network and were complicit in these ongoing human rights violations and crimes. "I don't know which was worse," one stolen baby victim told us.

The main targets of this mafia?

Single mothers, the working class, the uneducated, the abused, the already victimized. In short, those that could hardly defend themselves.

No small enterprise, evidence continues to mount which places the number of stolen babies at well over 300,000. Now multiply that number by dozens, each of which represents all the family members victimized. Next, include all the thousands of stolen babies we are only now beginning to realize are walking around all over the globe not even knowing they are not who they think, who they have been told they are and in a nation, Spain, of only 46 million or so, and you begin to grasp just how vast this criminal network, this mafia is in reality.

While many stolen babies were sold in Spain, thousands more were illegally smuggled out of the country. Spain became known on the black market as the "baby factory to the world."(5) Spanish babies were taken to places like the USA, Puerto Rico, Mexico, Argentina, Chile, anywhere where there was a demand the network ensured there was a supply. For the right price.

Today, through easy access to new and affordable DNA technology and testing, some of these stolen babies, now adults, are beginning to discover the truth. Many have yet to even suspect that they too, were victimized at birth. This is their story too.

Is this all some historical artifact? Perhaps, a terrible chapter of a distant, dictatorial past?

Hardly.

As we'll soon see, while this baby stealing mafia may have started in the aftermath of the Spanish Civil War for punitive and Nazi-inspired eugenic reasons, it didn't stop or even slow down as the decades passed. No, it actually got worse.

But before we go any further, overwhelmingly, stolen baby victims across Spain, now adults, do not want to be known only as faceless or nameless statistics or by their case file numbers.

With that in mind, we honor their request now by briefly getting to know just a few of the thousands across Spain who are searching for justice, as real people. Just like you and me.

Ascensión was a lot like many other children her age. She liked books, didn't like school that much, enjoyed her friends and adored her father. An only child of much older parents, she always knew she was "Daddy's Girl" but respected and obeyed her Mom, who was the stricter of the two.

When Ascen was just 10 years old, her father fell ill. She felt bad they couldn't spend as much time together as before but looked forward to the day when he would get better. Soon, she hoped, things would be just as they were before. Sadly, that day never arrived. Ascensión came home from school one afternoon to find family and adults she didn't know gathered at her house. The mood was somber and tense. "Don't go into the bedroom she was warned." But like most 10-year old kids she did just the opposite. There, she found her beloved father lying in repose on the bed. "The body was still warm" she recalls. Sobbing and overcome with grief, a trusted Aunt, Dolores, entered the room and snapped, "Why are you crying, you stupid little girl?"

Through her tears, Ascensión looked up at her Aunt in bewilderment. "That man," her Aunt continued, "he wasn't even your father, you were adopted."

Years later, Ascensión, now an adult and a mother herself, would discover that her Father was a member of the *Falange*, a feared, brutal and elite military unit which served the dictator Franco. (6) As a result of a private investigation she also became convinced that she was stolen from her biological mother as a baby and sold to whom she grew up thinking were her real parents. And who facilitated the illegal adoption? Ascen says evidence she possesses clearly shows who it was, and she said so on television in Spain.

Why then, is Ascen, a stolen baby victim, and not the guilty party facing jail time for coming forward with the truth?

Paquita was, as she puts it "no shrinking daisy."

As a young woman about to give birth she was told by her doctor that she was "tough." He told Paquita that he liked women who were tough and not "whiners" like so many of the pregnant women he saw each day. As she sat waiting in a small room at a hospital in Alicante, Spain, her water broke. She knew it was only a matter of moments before her delivery and she called out for help. Like a butcher at a New York City deli the nurse yelled back, "What is your number?" Paquita replied, "47." Then "wait your time and don't complain" she was told.

After finally hearing her number called, Paquita was delighted to deliver not one but two newborn babies. Twin girls. She was given permission to hold one of her newborn babies while the attending nurses kept the other one away from her. Later, as the nurses held both babies to bathe them, she heard one exclaim, "look at this one, how cute, but look at this one, how ugly."

Not long afterwards, one of the nurses approached Paquita with some shocking news. One of the babies, "the cute one" had

9

died. No explanation, no details. No opportunity to see the baby. "You are young," she was told, "you can always have more."

When Paquita's own mother came by to visit her that afternoon, she gripped her hand and pleaded with her, "Please, Mama, take my baby out of here before they kill her too."

Later, when Paquita and her husband worked up the courage to open the tiny box in which the hospital had supposedly placed their dead twin baby girl, they were again confronted with shocking news.

Clara was only a girl of 15 when she became a new mother. Already a victim of domestic abuse at the hands of an alcoholic parent, Clara was under the custodial control of the state as she suffered through a pregnancy with devastating physical side-effects. On the day she was to give birth, she recalls being placed not in an ambulance but inexplicably, in the backseat of a taxi. She was handed what looked like an aspirin. "Take this," she was told, "it will relax you." The next thing Clara recalls was waking up in a hospital clinic bed already having given birth. "You had complications," she was curtly informed. The baby boy you had died. And you can't stay here."

Shortly after giving birth and being informed that her baby had died, in shock and bleeding, Clara was, in her words, "put out into the streets with nothing."

Contemplating suicide at a train station in Barcelona, she was inspired by a stranger that helped remind a young Clara that life was worth living and to see through the darkness of the moment to a brighter future.

Years later, Clara, now married with children of her own, recalls getting a call which she initially thought was a cruel, tasteless joke. "Your baby didn't die," she was told. "In fact, you had a girl not a boy and she has been looking for you."

After fainting, Clara righted herself with the help of her husband. What followed next makes most television "soap operas" or *telenovelas* seem tame by comparison. Despite threats against her and her family, Clara vows to never be silenced in her relentless pursuit for justice. Even if it means unmasking a well-known, high-ranking Spanish cabinet minister whom she asserts, lied and defrauded her when she was a legal ward of the state.

Paqui Bria or simply 'Paqui,' as her family called her, was called something far different by her classmates. Something cruel. *Puta* or "whore of the street" they would call her. Adding that she would never know who her real parents were. Coming home in tears one day, Paqui asked her mother if there was any truth to what the kids were saying at school. Any truth that she was, as the kids called her, *hija de puta* "the daughter of a whore" and that she didn't even know her real parents. Ignore them she was told. Kids can be mean. It's all just lies.

But the insults and questions about her own identity persisted. Finally, soon after her 15th birthday, her mother admitted what Paqui had slowly begun to believe. She was adopted. End of story. But the "truth" her mother admitted to was not quite the whole truth. Nor was it the end of the story. There was more. Years later, as she was about to be married, Paqui requested a number of official documents to legally establish her formal name and family lineage. What she found out continues to shape her adult life and fuels her drive to uncover the full truth. Once and for all. "No matter how the story ends," Paqui says.

Though they have never met, **Raquel** and **Magaly** are forever connected. They share a unique bond that goes all the way back to when they were babies, and both were under the care of the *Inclusa*. This is a notorious orphanage in Madrid which has faced numerous allegations of fraud, deception and facilitation of stolen baby adoptions over the last several decades. Both Raquel and

Magaly were labeled as "abandoned" babies prior to being adopted. Today, both have uncovered evidence which strongly disputes this claim by the *Inclusa*.

Raquel started looking for her biological mother as a teenager. Little did she know that some 30 years later she would still be trying to uncover the truth about her adoption from Spain and subsequent, illegal transport to the USA. Now, married with children of her own and a resident of Panama City, Florida, Raquel feels it deep within her that she must find her real Mom and knows that time is running out. But as she boarded a commercial flight to Spain in the Spring of 2019, even she, had no idea what she would say to the woman she now believed was her biological mother. That is, if and, when, she was permitted to meet her in person.

When we met her in Puerto Rico where she has lived since being brought from Spain as a baby, Magaly told us that as she began to dig into her own past, she found one *mentira* or lie after another after another. After much discussion and deliberation, she decided to share her story with the public for the first time. Before a live television audience in San Juan, Puerto Rico and with Mara by her side, she took a deep breath and slowly began to answer the host's question, "Are you really a stolen baby from Spain?"

This same question has haunted **Ted**, an American living in Oklahoma for years. He continues his search which, with the help of new DNA testing, has him ever so close to possibly meeting his biological mother from Spain for the first time. But there's a catch.

After being deceived by the nuns at a notorious clinic in Madrid to give up her newborn baby, **Susan** had given up ever seeing her baby again. But her daughter, **Julia**, now an adult, was determined to find her real mother. Today, nearly four decades later, mother and daughter have exchanged poignant letters for the first time. A possible reunion was soon planned with the help of a professional mediator but then these things don't always go as planned.

Mercedes, it seemed, was destined to be a blessed mother of a newborn baby girl. For she was giving birth on May the 7th better known as Holy Mother's Day in Spain. But while the Catholic Church revered Mary, the original blessed virgin mother, current flesh and blood mothers like Mercedes were viewed far differently. Sister Pura, or "Pure" in Spanish, the head of the Francisco Franco hospital in Madrid where Mercedes gave birth, would herself be accused of multiple counts of baby stealing and illegal adoptions in the ensuing years. As it turned out, destiny was no match for human greed and sin.

Despite being told she was crazy, Mercedes remained convinced that she and her baby born on Mother's Day and stolen from her would someday be reunited. Some 40 years later, she may have her optimism rewarded.

Francisco, with his daughter and the beloved family pet, Lolo, by his side, recounted how, he, had in fact, been declared dead as a baby. He even showed us his death certificate. "They made a mistake," he said, "but not just the obvious one." As we leaned forward, he explained. He had a twin sister, and when they stole her from his real parents, as twin baby girls were especially coveted, part of the typical cover-up was to then declare the baby being stolen as having died at birth or shortly thereafter. "But they made out the death certificate in my name by mistake."

As an adult he continued to search for his stolen, twin sister. Along the journey he was joined by a partner. "Both my wife, Victoria and I, are siblings of stolen babies…It was a bond we shared that could never be broken."

Though losing his beloved wife to cancer not too long ago, Francisco or simply Paco to friends, along with their daughter Victoria (named after her mother), continue to keep searching

13

despite the passage of time. "We know of no better way to honor her memory than to never give up. But it gets harder and harder as each day passes."

In *Valencia*, **Antonio** and **Rosa** are both looking for siblings of stolen babies and happened to meet during their separate searches for the truth. Now married, they join fellow victims here throughout the year at rallies to try and raise awareness and let other victims know they are not alone. **María Jesús** is one such victim. She was told as a young mother that her baby was "healthy inside of her but when he entered the atmosphere he evaporated."

In *Sevilla*, to try and cope with the pain of her baby boy being stolen from her, **Lidia** has written a book and a play detailing the ongoing struggle. She leads an association of fellow victims to demand justice. **Alfonso**, a stolen baby himself, heads another association, also in Sevilla, to help spread the word and attract support. "It is not easy. It is often very hard. And sadly, many of the mothers are growing old and time is running short." **Ñoñi**, joined one such rally in Sevilla recently. She has found her stolen baby sister. But her mother is fearful of confronting her daughter. Afraid of the new trauma such a startling discovery might cause. Together, they finally came to a difficult decision.

In *San Sebastián*, a woman gestures with arms wide open. "Where is my baby?" she asks. "Here?" "Maybe there?" "What about over there?"

Andone has been fighting for years to find out the truth about her stolen baby. While the official word is her baby died shortly after birth and was buried in a cemetery in San Sebastian there is no grave, no tombstone, not even a simple marker of where the supposedly dead baby was buried. She pushes on, convinced the truth is out there somewhere, beyond the lies she has been told.

14

In *Madrid*, **Luis** raises a banner proclaiming support for all victims like himself as he searches for his baby brother on behalf of his now deceased mother.

In *Málaga*, **Encarna** tells an incredible tale of having her baby taken at birth only to discover nearly 30 years later, by chance and social media, that her long-lost daughter is alive and looking for her biological mother.

In *Barcelona*, **Dolores**, now 93, continues to search for her stolen baby boy. By her side is one of her grown sons who dutifully carries the papers they say clearly shows the deception by the hospital. He vows to carry on the fight once his mother is no longer able to.

In *Benidorm*, everything was fine for **Soledad and Ángel** and their baby boy until Soledad made the "mistake" of having her other two children visit their baby brother at the hospital the day they were to take him home. Suddenly, the nurse's attitude changed when she saw the children. Visiting time was over now, she declared. That night, they got a call, the baby boy had got sick and died, so badly decomposed they could not see him. Of course, all lies as they discovered later.

In *Alicante*, **Laura's** search for her own stolen baby recently came to a stunning end when she presided over a judicially ordered exhumation of the grave of her supposed dead baby. What she found should never be something any mother or anyone for that matter, should ever have to experience.

Does this seem like a lot of stolen baby victims still searching for answers? For justice?

Incredibly, what we've shared so far doesn't even begin to scratch the surface.

Coming next, in the *Introduction*, we detail just how we plan to help you, the reader, navigate this still unfolding and evolving human rights story.

15

As for us, we will do more than just scratch the surface of this ongoing human rights violation in the coming pages. We will go wherever the facts take us. Justice seems to demand it and certainly, all the stolen baby victims and their loved ones deserve this and more.

Introduction
How Would Any of Us React?

"We simply want to know where our babies are and give them a big hug before we die."- Lidia, a Sevilla victim

What you are about to read has not been embellished nor fictionalized. It is real. As shocking as some of it, maybe even most of it, may be, these are all true events that happened to actual people. And what's worse, it's not about some distant and long since forgotten past. While systematic baby stealing began in Spain just before the Spanish Civil War ended in 1939, we are still hearing of new cases as recently as the year 2000 that are only now being investigated. (1)

As we talked with so many of these victims, we couldn't help but wonder how we would feel or react if we were in their shoes.

For that matter, how would any of us feel, if our baby was taken from us shortly after birth and never given back?

How would any of us react if we were told our baby had died shortly after birth only to later found out we had been lied to and our baby had not really died but had been sold to strangers?

And now, this baby, all grown-up, was living somewhere unknown to us. What would we feel, knowing we had been deceived by those we trusted the most in life-doctors, nurses, priests, nuns, social workers, caregivers, our elected officials? Like a bottomless well, the corruption runs deeper than anyone can fully fathom.

The actual mothers and fathers who continue to search for their stolen babies still feel a deep sense of betrayal and deception. The passage of time has not softened or healed their pain.

17

The babies, now adults, who have discovered the truth of their own origin, now realize that because of this passage of time their chance at ever being reunited with their biological parents or relatives is growing fainter by the day. They feel a sense of urgency, desperation and despair.

And everyone, directly or indirectly impacted by these human rights violations in Spain and across the globe share something in common- They all face a system determined to make sure that the truth stays dead and buried. Maybe worse, those culpable for such crimes against the rule of law and sins against humanity continue to escape punishment.

So, maybe, it's more accurate to say that all the victims we have spoken with these past several years are angry. They are outraged that such a crime could even happen in the first place and that the truth could then be hidden from them in plain sight. Many describe themselves as being victimized not once but twice.

Now, before we do our best to explain how and why this all started and why those in power want to keep the truth hidden, let's first get to know just a few of the many victims. Not just as nameless or faceless victims but as who they truly are- real people just like you and me with real lives. Only living with an unthinkable loss.

Through their sorrow and through their tears they want the world to know them not merely as victims but rather, as ordinary people trying to overcome extraordinary hurdles.

As one victim put it, "We aren't just a case in a file or a number on a page, we are no different than anyone else. We just want to be whole again."

Across Spain, to the west and east, north and south, no region or province or city or town or village seems immune from this tragedy. No family seems completely unaffected by the stealing of babies that has now gone on for over six decades.

In fact, no part of Spain has been left untouched or untainted by these crimes. In researching this book and the documentary film by the same name, we conducted over 300 interviews with Spaniards who all shared eerily similar stories of deceptions, lies and fraud. Of trust being betrayed by doctors, nurses, priests and politicians. Of cases being closed by prosecutors despite overwhelming evidence to the contrary. Of an endless search that leads only to more lies, more deception and more frustration.

And yet, this number, 300, by no means insignificant, still barely begins to show the full scope of the crimes and human rights violations inflicted throughout Spain and beyond.

Reliable estimates have conservatively placed the number of stolen baby victims at over 300,000. But many believe this number is even higher. And the number grows exponentially in terms of the families and friends these thefts have and continue to affect, to harm and the emotional scars left in their wake. (2)

These are crimes unlimited in their capacity to cause pain and suffering across all ages, all genders, all generations. These are crimes unlimited in their moral depravity.

"How could any human treat another so inhumanely?" wondered another victim.

In the coming chapters you will get to know up close and personal several of the victims and their ongoing cases. These are their stories in their own words. And we are grateful for their trust and willingness to open-up to us and now you, about their struggle. Many have been honest about the fear they feel in coming forward. They fear retaliation for simply telling the world the truth. That their own government, their church, their caregivers lied to them, covered-up the truth and now block their path to justice. They fear they will lose their jobs, their livelihoods, maybe even their own lives as they pursue the truth.

But still, they come forward.

"What else can they take?" asks María, a victim, "that they have not already taken?"

Chapter 1 sheds some light on how and why baby stealing in Spain started and the obstacles that were put in place decades ago by the government and the church which still hinder victims discovering the truth and getting justice today.

Chapter 2 shares powerful and poignant stories from several *madres* (mothers) who still search for their babies taken away from them at birth. Their stories are unsettlingly similar, it's as if those who violated them all followed the same script or manual.

Chapter 3 shares stories that are quite common among the actual stolen babies, now adults. Whether looking for a sibling or their biological parents, they face an all too familiar path of lies, deception, falsified records, and a well-meaning but largely impotent or outright hostile government, depending on which political party holds a majority at any given time. Despite holding in their hands overwhelming evidence, they all feel frustration as their cases are closed (*archivado*) by prosecutors who claim their own hands are tied. They also share similar stories and experience similar frustrations. They all realize that time is not on their side.

Chapter 4 takes an even more in-depth look at two victims whom you have already "met" briefly and their cases. The first, Ascen, continues to face possible jail time and steep fines for, as she asserts, simply telling the truth. The second, Clara, is at first glance, a classic case of a single girl betrayed by those around her but with a profound twist-she points an accusing finger at, among others, a powerful and currently high-ranking Spanish official. Soon, you will get to know these courageous women and their search for truth and justice.

Chapters 5 and 6 shares the story of Enrique Vila, a contributing author to this book and a victim and advocate for stolen babies as well as, for the first time in English, some of his more dramatic cases so that an even wider audience may come to know the details of these struggles. And for the first-time in any publication or language, Mr. Vila has allowed previously confidential and untold details to now be made public for the good of all victims. You will come to know the struggles faced by Julia and her biological mother Susan, as well as María and her biological daughter Ana, and finally, the story of Ted, a baby born in Spain and taken to America.

Chapter 7 provides important insight into the political, legal and social hurdles which all victims continue to face in their search for justice. Here, you will meet Carmen, a former nun with the Daughters of Charity, as she provides details about what really happened in notorious clinics like Santa Cristina, Francisco González de Tena, a well-known sociologist and author in Spain, Pablo Rosser, a historical memory and cultural expert from Alicante and María José Esteso, an investigative journalist and author who has written extensively on the subject of stolen babies of Spain.

In Chapter 8 we share the incredible story of Inés Madrigal who came to national and international prominence recently as the accuser of the notorious gynecologist Dr. Vela. Based in part on three separate, private interviews we conducted with Inés as well as court documents and footage we filmed during the trial, we believe you may come away as we did, with a newfound respect and insight as to the courage and persistence it took just to finally bring someone to court over the crimes depicted in this book and in the film.

In Chapter 9 we chronicle the brief yet significant actual trial of Dr. Vela, which we were able to film on location and were granted behind-the-scenes access. Here, we also sat down for a final time with the accuser, Inés Madrigal, and got her reaction right after the trial ended and her thoughts as to what the verdict means going forward for all victims.

In Chapter 10 we pull back a bit and "pan wide" to look at the current global epidemic of baby stealing and trafficking. Every month we are contacted by more victims, some who were stolen as babies in Spain and are trying to find family in Spain, some stolen in Spain and smuggled to other nations like the USA. Still, some others who were stolen as babies in different nations like Serbia, but all who tell us similar stories of lies, betrayal and endless struggles for the truth. There is reason for hope though and some progress has been made due to pressure applied by organizations like the European Union, the Council of Europe and the United Nations. We are thankful for leaders like UK Member of the European Parliament Jude Kirton-Darling who is committed to helping her fellow countrywoman Ruth Appleby and stolen baby victims everywhere get justice. Once and for all.

Over the last 4 years, as we traveled across Spain filming and conducting interviews with victims, we kept asking ourselves and really, anybody who would listen- Will anyone ever be punished for these crimes?

Afterall, hopes for justice had been raised and dashed in Spain before. A few years ago, a notorious nun, Sister María Gómez Valbuena of the Santa Cristina clinic, was indicted for baby stealing but she died just days after she took the Spanish equivalent of pleading the Fifth (The Right to Not Declare) before formally facing charges. Few details of her death were shared with the public and despite it being viewed as a sin in her own Catholic Church, her body was cremated immediately, and, as a result, no official autopsy was conducted. Incidents like this only continue to fan the flames of conspiracy theorists that Sister María and others similarly accused are not truly dead as officially declared but have all been allowed to disappear to elude justice.

Maybe things were about to change.

As the trial of Dr. Vela gained more media attention in Spain in the summer of 2018, hope once again began to slowly rise among many victims that finally, someone would be held accountable for these horrific crimes. Vela, a retired gynecologist was alleged to have facilitated the illegal adoptions and theft of hundreds even thousands of babies and selling them over a span of 50 years and had, up to this point, eluded justice.

But this time his accuser came armed with evidence and not just hearsay.

Inés Madrigal, a clear spoken, determined mother and wife claimed she had actual proof that Vela had stolen her and given her "as a gift" to her adopted mother who was apparently introduced to Vela by a mutual friend, a Jesuit Priest.

Would this finally be the case that tore the top off the judicial box many victims felt trapped in?

You will get that answer soon enough. Promise.

We start though, at the end.

As the Spanish Civil War (1936-1939) was ending, the victors' dream of transplanting Nazi-style eugenics to Spain, to achieve a sort of "Spanish Master Race," was just starting to become a reality. And Spain would never again be the same.

23

Chapter 1
How We Got Here

Revenge and Reproduction.

Inspired by Nazi eugenics, which sought to create a supposed "master Aryan race" by eliminating the weakest, least able members of its society through controlled procreation and genetic engineering, Franco envisioned a similar eugenics strategy for a post-war Spain. With a sinister twist. (1)

This newly engineered Spanish race under Franco, would, in effect, be a return to the old and the traditional. A return to a time when Spain was admired, feared, and built an empire that spanned the globe. Instead of what he viewed as leftist radicalism and unhinged socialism, Spain would be restored to a unified Christian nation. A nation free of the secular, anti-Christ Republican radicals that had plagued it for decades. With Franco (The Savior) as its patriarch, traditional church values and the "proper" roles of men as dominant and women as subservient in everyday Spanish life would also be restored. The progressive gains for women and minorities before the war would be revoked. Wars, as historians remind us, do indeed have consequences.

And to accomplish this mission, this vision of a "new-old Spain" in a post-civil war Spain, he assigned his right-hand man, Antonio Vallejo-Nágera, the head of his military psychiatric services, to lead the way. The specifics of the plan called for the elimination of any remaining seeds of dissidence or opposition to the new regime. Vallejo-Nágera who had been studying Nazi eugenics since World War I had become a rabid believer in genetic engineering and an equally zealous Francoist. Just as Nazi eugenicists viewed the Weimar Republic (1918-1933) and its overt liberalism as a "sick organism" that had been allowed to "enter the bloodstream of Germany and to contaminate it," Vallejo-Nágera believed that the Spanish Civil War was a necessary evil to "purify the spirit and soul of Spain from the infectious disease of liberalism." (2) And just as Nazi eugenicists sought to apply strategic genetic engineering to "purify the Aryan race of all impure and weak elements" so that a new, stronger Germany could rise from the ashes of war, Vallejo-Nágera sought to use similar eugenics to "cure the disease of red liberalism and allow *El Caudillo* (Franco, the Warlord) to unify and completely re-Christianize Spain."

He convinced Franco that victories on the battlefield would prove hollow if the disease (communism) that "entered the bloodstream of a Christian Spain" were ever allowed to "sicken the patient, our beloved Spain" again. Franco agreed and placed full political and military support behind Vallejo-Nágera's Nazi-inspired scheme to achieve this goal. Consequently, even before the fighting of the civil war ended, Vallejo-Nágera had already begun to test his perverse eugenics theories on real, live humans in captivity.

Describing captured Republican women being held in prisons during the war as "degenerate animals" who were "unfit to reproduce," Vallejo-Nágera sought "scientific proof" to support his Nazi-inspired racism. And while he never actually had any direct contact with any of these women, he presumptively declared them as carriers of a "contagious, social disease" and concluded, based on his highly flawed scientific observations and data collected, that any reproductive "seed" originating from these "sub-humans" must be eliminated. (3)

Consequently, the brutal treatment of these women in prison was justified as part of an "elegant nationalist" plan to save Spain from widespread, loathsome, degeneracy. And since these captured Republican women were viewed by Nationalists as "sub-

25

human" no act or punishment against them, could, by definition, be too vile or excessive. Women had their heads shaved to rid them of any outward femininity and were frequently beaten, tortured and raped by their male captors who called them "*putas, rojas, feas y peladas*" (whores, reds, ugly and bald). (4)

The goal of the Nationalists was to humiliate, degrade and socially isolate these sub-human females. The notion was that even if some survived and became free again, each would be forever broken and pose no risk of "contaminating" a newly purified, Spanish society. Any females who became pregnant in prison or who entered prison pregnant and later gave birth would immediately be separated from their baby. How could such mentally deficient, unfit mothers be allowed to raise their babies in Franco's Spain? The answer? They could not and would not be allowed to do so. All for the greater good of this "new-old" Spain.

One of the only women to actually chronicle such brutality and abuse in these so-called "Franco's Prisons for Women" was Pilar Fidalgo. She was a Republican female held captive at *La Prisión de Madres Lactantes* (The Prison of Lactating Mothers) in Madrid. In her book, *A Young Mother in Franco's Prisons,* she wrote that there were dozens of women in a cell originally built for one adult inmate. She and her child, who had been captured together, at one point became seriously ill. The prison doctor, Pedro Almendral, she claims, told her that the only and best cure was simply to die, to simply do the right thing and kill herself and her child. She also writes that many of her fellow women prisoners were told by guards and even nuns to run away and escape, that this was their only way to survive. But when many did so and tried to escape, they were executed, shot in the back. Some were beaten and raped in front of other prisoners, first, as a message to the rest and then afterwards, killed. Bodies of these slain women were then stacked in open graves, many were then defecated and spat upon by guards.

Those, like Pilar, who did not run, were still beaten and raped by guards and even priests for their "cowardliness and degeneracy" at, you guessed it, not trying to escape. In effect, they were punished for not following orders, even though such orders were sure to get them killed anyway. Señora Fidalgo tells of priests and nuns who would then bring gifts and offer congratulations to the Nationalist Guards for their "zealous defense of the Holy Religion" and for "implementing the necessary suppression of these vile, degenerate, female prisoners." (5)

By the time the Spanish Civil War officially ended on March 28, 1939, the Nationalists' plan to restore Spain as a unified and Christian nation free of Republican women and their impure offspring, had already begun in earnest. What had worked in prison could now be applied on a much larger scale in civilian life. And to do so would take a full, collaborative effort of the state, military and church apparatus.

Fortunately for Vallejo-Nágera, at Franco's behest, he had full authority and unlimited resources at his command. Importantly, he also enjoyed the active participation of the Catholic Church. Now, to paraphrase the French, it was a matter of ensuring the devil was indeed in the details.

The plan was two-pronged. First, it was imperative to show no mercy at all to the "sick and perverse enemy." The Nationalists must punish and destroy any and all survivors suspected of being sympathetic to the vanquished Spanish Republicans. A true Nationalist victory led by Franco, Vallejo-Nágera declared, "would be nothing short of the complete annihilation of large numbers if not all Republicans and the total humiliation and terrorization of any of its surviving population." And so, punish and destroy their once fellow Spaniards but now vanquished enemies, they did. With a vengeance. Even today, Spanish authorities are still discovering additional, unmarked mass graves of those executed after the war by Franco. Reliable estimates now place the human toll of the civil war and its aftermath at between 600,000 to nearly 1 million. A stunning number given that at the time Spain's entire population was only about 25 million. (6)

For Vallejo-Nágera, though, it was a small price to pay for the desired outcome. As he argued, "reds were degenerates and if they were allowed to breed, they would enfeeble the Spanish race...they had to be exterminated like rats." His Nazi-inspired eugenics policy demanded nothing less. (7)

However, Vallejo-Nágera and Franco also realized that literally executing every single Republican or those still sympathetic to their cause now and to the future was a practical impossibility. And even if it could somehow be made possible, doing so would weaken their capacity to rebuild Spain, a nation still very much dependent on manual labor and human capital.

So, if this supposed "red gene" could not be completely prevented from passing from deficient and perverse Republicans to its offspring through "unholy procreation" then the next best thing, the second prong of the plan, would be to isolate the "red gene" offspring from its procreators. Cut off from any poisonous influence from its biological parents, this "red carrier" (the baby) could then be "re-programmed" and indoctrinated by more suitable parents and Nationalist families loyal to Franco. (8)

Applying the science of eugenic racism to Spain to once and for all "cleanse the Spanish race" also involved ridding the nation of all other environmental factors that could "incubate and nurture the red gene." Such factors included allowing unfit mothers to reproduce and allowing any influences outside of those sanctioned by the Holy Church to "infect" families. From the Nationalist

28

perspective, cleansing the race by elimination of these factors had already proven to be possible. They pointed to their treatment of women and their babies born to them in prison during the war as proof positive. What worked inside these prisons would then just need to be expanded to work outside the prison walls and across Spain.

For example, the physical and emotional humiliation and "purification" of "degenerate" women continued unabated in a post-war society. Many women deemed to be promiscuous, of ill-repute, atheist, or suspected of being Republican sympathizers were forced to endure so-called "Walks of Shame." Similar in nature to the abuse which women in prisons suffered, here, civil police stripped women naked, shaved their heads and forced them to drink castor oil and then marched them through the main streets and town squares where they lived, as their neighbors looked on. Many defecated uncontrollably, due to the castor oil, and were then thrown to the ground in mud to complete the depiction of a woman who is filthy and must be purged of her evil, her wantonness and her demonic communism ("purgando el demonio del comunismo"). Frequently, these "walks" ended with the death of the purged woman. But at least the "red beast" within had been ousted for all to see. (9)

In time then, if, all went according to their own "master plan," any "mentally deficient socialist tendencies" would then eventually die off and never return. And if it also took "redistributing" thousands of Spanish babies from their "morally deficient" and "ideologically bankrupt" biological parents to do what was best for Spain then so be it. As Vallejo-Nágera often told his fellow Spaniards, "What we do is, after all, God's will on earth." (10)

And who knew better what was "God's will" than the Catholic Church?

29

It stood steeple-ready, able and quite willing to re-emerge as a key institution of patriarchal control and national authority now that the "mentally deficient Socialists" were no longer in charge. Consequently, forcibly taking babies from their Republican or "Red" biological mothers and giving them to proper, devout Catholic, Nationalist mothers and fathers was not viewed as sinning by many clergy in the church. Quite the opposite, many believed they were saving Spain from sin.

Fully clothed then in the cloak of charity and grace while they took babies away from their mothers, the church soon realized that some mothers were simply easier to "save" from themselves and their newborn babies than others. Through formal and informal channels, the church became adept at identifying vulnerable, impoverished, desperate pregnant women who had few viable options left in life.

Once identified, initial contact was made with promises of care, protection and salvation waiting for the mother-to-be at the other end of this outreached hand. Through its church-run hospices and clinics, they (nuns and anointed volunteers) could then help deliver newborn babies and as a trusted caregiver, were in a perfect position to then take the babies away from their "unfit" mothers and place them in proper and "fit" Nationalist homes.

Several nuns who were heads of such clinics like Sister María of the Santa Cristina Clinic in Madrid, Sister Aurora of the *Casa Cuna* in Valencia, or Sister Pura of *Tu Casa*, developed, and managed a coercive network of government officials, social workers, caregivers and other associates over several decades to ensure a smooth, albeit, criminal, enterprise of baby stealing and reallocation. In the next chapter we will see examples of this as told to us by mothers who were taken in with the promise of protection and kindness only to later realize they were deceived. And that their babies were long gone.

From first-hand accounts, and personal journals and diaries as well as some tireless investigative research by journalists like María José Esteso we now know that identifying, segregating and isolating vulnerable women was, by design, not that difficult in post-war Spain. Stemming back to practices which began in Franco's prisons under Vallejo-Nágera, known Republican women and anyone suspected of being a Republican loyalist were shunned, dismissed from work, forbidden to attend school or to pursue any education. Consequently, such emotional, physical and economic isolation left many women with no choice but to resort to prostitution or ironically, the convent to serve as nuns, as their only paths of survival. This contrived and overt isolation was then viewed by Nationalists and the church as a "marker" of innate inferiority and "deviant red behavior." Damned if they did, damned if they did not. (11)

One of the questions we had when we first began interviewing some of the female victims was "Why did so few of the victims ever protest or seek assistance if they had suspicions of being exploited by the church in such a criminal way"?

The answer soon became clear. Often, the victim, due to poor or no education and through years of conditioning to unquestioningly trust the church and those with prestige and power like doctors or nurses, simply never suspected that they were, in fact, being exploited. Deceived. Betrayed. In those rare instances when victims did suspect or even have evidence of such exploitation and human rights violations at the hands of the church and the hospital where could they actually go to get help? Who could they trust to tell their story to? Would anyone, except maybe a similarly shunned, helpless and isolated victim even believe their story?

For many victims it was inconceivable that those whom they were brought up since children to believe in, trust, even revere could commit such unspeakable acts in violation of their sacred, holy vows. So inconceivable in fact, that many doubted their own instincts, intuition, even evidence. And when they finally discovered the awful truth or accepted what they knew all along, many kept it to themselves and suffered in silence. As Lidia, whom you will meet soon, noted to us, "I never thought there might be more like me out there. I believed for years I was the only one this happened to."

The symbiotic post-war alliance between Franco and the Catholic Church quickly forged into an unbreakable bond, each providing a necessary service for the acquisition and consolidation of power for the other. The church was restored to its self-appointed, proper place in the formal schooling and care of the population and fully embraced its role in helping to implement Vallejo-Nágera's plan. The church would continue to help identify, isolate, and then exploit vulnerable females as a means of taking away their babies to help ensure Franco's Nationalist purity. It was either side with the Godless communists on the left who tried to weaken the church under the Second Republic of Spain (1931-1939) or stand with the new savior of a re-Christianized Spain in Francisco Franco.

For the church the choice was clear. For his part, Franco would provide political and legal cover to help ensure that the church would ascend once again to its rightful place. They were convinced that no less than the very soul of Spain was at stake. Unlike during the Second Republic, there would be no church burnings, no repudiation of Christianity, no false claims of any other religious idol under Franco, only Catholicism.

Like the Third Reich, whose Nazi founders envisioned would last into perpetuity, Franco took swift steps after the civil war to help ensure that his new regime would last "forever" as well. A number of laws heavily influenced by Vallejo-Nágera's brand of

32

Nazi eugenics were passed, each aimed at codifying the reshaping of this new, Spanish society. For example, in December of 1941, Franco legalized the ability of the state and church to officially change the birth names of all orphans, of all children born in prisons and now out, and of any future babies born to Republican females in prison. During the filming of our documentary, it struck one of our crew members who had never visited Spain before of how many women were named after the Virgin Mary and how many men after Joseph. In large part, this is why. (12)

Franco also reinstated the *Patronato de Protección de la Mujer* but endowed it with a far more sinister and controlling mission than before. The official purpose, according to the decree of November 6, 1941 was to protect the moral dignity of women, especially of young women to prevent their exploitation, help them avoid any deviation into vice and to educate them in accordance with the teachings of Catholicism.

But to victims these *Patronatos*, under the cover of this official decree, became the exploiters, the predators who would prey upon helpless, single, young women, controlling their lives and taking their babies. Headed by Franco's wife, Carmen Polo de Franco, the *Patronatos* became the danger from which victims needed protection.

In practice, these *Patronatos*, organized across Spain, served as a network aimed at closely monitoring and scrutinizing female behavior and activity in public to ensure that the norms of the church were not being contravened in any way. The belief was that such scrutiny was needed to protect Christian society from the natural "degeneracy" and "wantonness" of Republican women. A degeneracy and danger of which Vallejo-Nágera had chronicled in the war prisons and warned against. In executing its mission, officials organized street raids, rounding up any female deemed to be deviant in dress or behavior and encouraged and rewarded

33

anyone, even family members, who alerted the *Patronatos* about such behavior or attitudes being exhibited in private life. Often it took only one such complaint, substantiated or not, to get a young girl now deemed "unruly" to be assigned to one of these *Patronato* care centers.

Once assigned, voluntarily leaving the centers was all but impossible. All female minors who entered the center no longer enjoyed the same rights as before. Their parents lost legal custody over them while the *Patronato* immediately assumed all legal and custodial rights of the child.

Unwed, single girls who became pregnant were most frequently assigned to such *Patronatos* as a means of keeping her "degeneracy" private. But this privacy came with a high price. Once her baby was delivered within the confines of the *Patronato* and its staff, the forcible or deceptive taking of the baby away from the new mother was easy to do and extremely hard to fight or challenge.

Complicating matters was the fact that many of these unwed, single mothers were assigned to the *Patronatos* by their parents not just to maintain privacy but also as a means to curry favor with the new regime and avoid punishment for not coming forward voluntarily. It was already bad enough to be parents of a child who became pregnant out of wedlock in violation of Franco's decrees but to be caught "hiding it" could lead to banishment, even death.

While many girls ended up interned at a *Patronato*, for a variety of reasons, including whether or not she had been "touched" or "untouched" (a virgin or not) or had engaged in illicit acts like prostitution, they all had to submit to a strict and unyielding daily regimen. Designed to stamp out her natural "degeneracy" and "wantonness" and to eliminate her connection to any "red gene" she carried, the *Patronatos* became, for many women, a nightmare without end.

As one victim, a former *Patronato* survivor who gave birth and had her baby taken away from her, shared, "I had few options and thought this would be a place of salvation and hope. Instead, it was a place of betrayal and abuse. I was not the only one."

But what about those stolen babies who, whether they were born in a *Patronato*, hospital or clinic of some kind, had not, for whatever reason, been placed with a "fit" Nationalist family by their third birthday? (13)

In Franco's post-war Spain these "rejected" babies we interviewed, now, adults well into their 70s and 80s recall an even worse kind of upbringing at the hands of the church and state.

According to law, if a baby had already been "poisoned by its degenerate and unfit parents" and had reached the age of 3 and proved difficult to place with proper, Nationalist families, a different solution was established. A solution which also helped ensure the perpetuity of the Franco regime and the church.

What was this "alternate" solution?

It was to immediately begin the training of these children to both save them from the sins of their parents and to better serve their "saviors" by becoming priests, nuns or Christian soldiers for Franco's army. Each would then be "blessed" to serve the "higher purpose" of preserving and protecting state and church.

The means to this solution?

The creation of the *Auxilio Social* institutions across Spain.

These *Auxilio Social* institutions, varnished with a patina of an altruistic façade, were actually a favorite instrument of societal control in post-war Spain. These institutions helped consolidate and mark Franco's domination over the vanquished. Social psychiatrists believe that any state-sponsored torture must "mark the victim," both actually and figuratively. For example, Jews that managed to escape the brutality of their Nazi captors were forever branded as "inferior" and "less human" by the marks and symbols burned into their body. Figuratively, each was forever emotionally branded or scarred by a result of the experience. Similarly, these *Auxilios* permanently branded the children who were under their "care" through physical and emotional torture and abuse. More akin to prisons than anything social, these *Auxilios* were described by many of its now adult survivors as "simply a living hell." Children were forced to endure daily verbal and physical assaults, indescribable brutality and beatings, whippings and even sexual assault and rape for alleged misbehaviors. Many were given barely enough food and water to survive. Ensuring that Vallejo-Nágera's eugenic policies were enforced, children were instructed to hate their biological parents and to openly reject and renounce them and to, instead, profess their love of Franco and to worship the Catholic Church. This daily exercise of hating their parents and expressing devotion to church and state through prayer took up anywhere from 4-6 hours each day.

According to one such survivor of a typical *Auxilio Social*, Uxeno Álvarez, all the brutality, punishments and ruthlessness he endured at the hands of his "teachers" ill-prepared him for adult life. "No me enseñaron nada… ni un oficio ni nada. Eso sí, yo me sé todos los himnos épicos de Falange: "Cara al sol", "Yo tenía un camarada" …Y luego todos los de la iglesia: "Padre nuestro", "Yo pecador me confieso", los Diez Mandamientos…" (They didn't teach me anything… not a trade or anything. Of course, I know all the epic hymns of the Falange: "Face to the sun," or "I had a comrade" ... And then all of the church devotionals: "Our Father", "I sinner I confess", the Ten Commandments…all of them, worthless. (14)

But as part of the new plan for Spain, these *Auxilios* and the role the Church played in their daily operations was exactly how it had been envisioned. The Catholic Church was re-emerging as a dominant and influential force in shaping future generations of

Spain. And, if children like Uxeno and Jose María recalled things differently, then again, so be it. As Vallejo-Nágera and his colleagues declared, "A pure and devout Catholic nation led by Franco was the only path to protect family, re-establish Spanish unity and rid the nation of the filth of international conspirators and collaborators." And the *Auxilios* was seen by the Nationalists as an integral stop along this righteous path. (15)

Besides the *Patronatos* and the *Auxilios* there was another instrument of monitoring, teaching and reinforcement of the new norms and standards in Franco's Spain. And in many ways this agency or section of government was the most zealous and ideological of them all. In fact, when it came to follow through on Vallejo-Nágera's eugenics policy, perhaps, no other arm of the new regime was as brutally efficient and loyal to the cause as was the *Sección Femenina de la Falange* (The female section of the Falange Party). (16)

Formed prior to the Spanish Civil War, the Falange Party housed some of the most extreme and fervent believers of all the Francoists. This section (*Sección Femenina*) was led by Pilar Primo de Rivera, the daughter of the former Spanish dictator, Miguel Primo de Rivera (1923-1930), and sister of José Antonio, founder of the Fascist *Falange Española*. Referred to as the *"Cuerpo de Divulgación"* (Body of Full Disclosure) (17) these women for Franco strictly monitored and enforced the eugenic policies under the new regime. These included; banning abortions, adherence to a "marriage mandate" for women prior to bearing any children, and a broad promulgation for all women to do what was necessary to avoid "wittingly or unwittingly" passing on the "red gene" to future generations.

Part of the mission of Primo de Rivera's *Sección Femenina* was to teach, indoctrinate and reinforce to a new Spain everyone's proper and approved role. Through mass communication and

37

promulgation of accepted behaviors the *Sección* got the good word out in part by presenting mandatory workshops, in-home teaching, counseling and published thousands of flyers, books and manuals with helpful titles like *How to Please your Husband* and *How to Have a Successful Marriage.* (18) These guides extolled the wisdom to women of never appearing to be smarter than her husband, being subservient at all times and embracing in and accepting her innate, inferiority. Their message to both women and girls was to be obedient, loyal and never overtly sexual or wanton. Marriage should reflect traditional and accepted Christian values.

In practice this meant that the Spanish man was returned to his rightful place of dominance over the inferior woman. Divorce was once again outlawed and if women misbehaved or displeased their husband then any necessary domestic beating or "re-conditioning" to ensure proper obedience was viewed as just. The *Sección* also played a key role in helping to identify and isolate especially vulnerable or wanton women, and worked closely with both the *Patronatos* and church run hospitals and clinics in coordinating the "reallocation" of "red babies" away from their "red mothers" and to Franco loyalists. (19)

And so, infused with religious and ideological fervor, the victor's dream of creating a Nazi-style "eugenics hierarchy" in post-war society was efficiently and ruthlessly implemented across Spain.

Vallejo-Nágera wrote about the "resounding success" Nationalist policies were enjoying and that he was even "more certain that the red gene" would soon die off" and that *El Caudillos'* (Franco's) legacy would live forever. (20)

Of course, anyone who disagreed with this assessment or was found to oppose this plan, anyone who questioned if their newborn babies had actually died at birth, anyone who chafed or hesitated

38

to ensure that "God's will" be done in Spain were, as one former Franco official told us, "executed or quickly made to disappear."

España es Diferente (Spain is Different)

Gradually though, by about the mid-1950s, the post-war, revolutionary flames that had burned so hot for so long, gradually began to recede into a more constant, slow burn. And with it, the sinister, Nazi-inspired eugenics which had for years fueled the initial baby stealing and reallocation also began to change and be driven by what crimes almost always seem to be driven by.

Greed.

An insatiable lust for profit. Baby stealing became a boom business in a newly emerging, post-war Spain. There seemed to be a bottomless demand for supply, for newborn Spanish babies, both within and outside its own borders. And those in the mafia network became fat, rich and happy. All at the expense of a trusting and painfully obedient society.

Like its new, consumer-oriented slogan, *España es Diferente* (Spain is Different) aimed at attracting more tourists with money to burn, Spain was indeed different. (21) No longer fully shuttered to the outside world, Spain under the dictator Franco began to open its doors to new business ventures and new capital investments. And black-market baby stealing was proving to be a lucrative business.

Those within this criminal network operated with impunity. They weren't above the law. They were the law.

This was a mafia which implicated doctors and nurses, revered priests and nuns, respected government leaders and bureaucrats. Its tentacles connected everyone from gravediggers to local bureaucrats to DNA laboratory technicians to "baby cabbies" or taxi-cab drivers paid to illegally transport stolen babies in-between so-called "stolen baby corridors" in Spain to high-profile cabinet-level officials to social workers to local police, politicians and prosecutors. Follow the breadcrumbs, one victim told us, and it will lead you all the way to the Pope perched on his throne in the Vatican and the secret adoption records kept there under lock and key.

Victims point an accusing finger over the last several decades at these individuals and more as all being part of this criminal network conceived for the purpose of stealing and selling their babies for profit. Either they took an active part or knew about the network and said and did nothing to stop it. "I don't know which was worse," asked María Jesús, who continues to search for two of her babies stolen some forty years ago.

The main targets of this for-profit mafia?

Single mothers, the working class, the uneducated, the abused, the already victimized. In short, those that were in no position to defend or protect themselves.

No small criminal enterprise, evidence continues to mount which places the number of stolen babies by this mafia at well over 300,000. Now multiply that number by dozens, each of which represents all the family members victimized. Next, include all the thousands of stolen babies we are only now beginning to realize are walking around all over the globe not even knowing they are not who they think, who they have been told they are, and in a nation, Spain, of only 46 million or so as of 2019, you begin to grasp just how vast this criminal network, this mafia is in reality. And how tragically broad their impact of crime has been on so many.

While most stolen babies were sold in Spain, thousands more were illegally smuggled out of the country. Spain became known on the black market as the "baby factory to the world." (22) Spanish babies were taken to places like the USA, Puerto Rico, Mexico, Venezuela, Brazil, Argentina and Chile. Wherever there was a demand the network ensured there was a supply. For the right price of course and no questions asked.

Today, through easy access to new and affordable DNA testing some of these stolen babies, now adults, are beginning to discover the truth of their own ancestry. Many have yet to even suspect that they too, were victimized at birth not knowing that family members are frantically searching for them. This is their story too.

Is all of this baby stealing some historical artifact? Something we can at least console ourselves with the fact it happened a long time under a dictator and can never happen again?

Hardly.

While this baby stealing mafia or network, aligned closely with the church may have started in the aftermath of the Spanish Civil War and did so for primarily, reasons of revenge and reproduction, it has not yet been fully dismantled. The powerful and the privileged continue to keep damaging records hidden and locked away from victims, cases continue to get closed by state prosecutors despite overwhelming evidence, elected officials continue to point to political and legal obstacles they claim tie their hands despite having the power to dismantle any and all such obstacles and the church remains mostly silent, promising only to hear victims in a respectful way. And while international pressure on Spain to once and for all confront these past crimes and make things right continues to rise, Spain's leaders, especially those conservative leaders seen as political descendants of Franco, remain steadfast in their opposition. Some have even gone so far as to claim it is all "merely an elaborate hoax" to try and extort money from the government. (23)

From our own research, private interviews and all those we filmed on record, we can say that if there is one commonality, one sentiment shared by every single victim, it is that no one wants any money for their pain and suffering. They want only to know the truth of what happened, to see justice done and mostly, they want, if, at all still possible, to be reunited with their loved ones before time runs out.

"Is this too much to ask for what was done to us?" asks one victim.

We'll get our answer in Chapter 2 where we get to know several of the stolen baby victims and their stories in their own words.

Chapter 2
Mothers Who Search

Before We Go Any Further...

You should know that the following cases are all true. Fact not fiction. All of them have been corroborated by some combination of official documents, hard evidence, witnesses, sworn testimony, affidavits and personal or familial memories and memorabilia. In many cases, what you are about to read involve all the above and more.

The stories in the following chapters have been chosen because in many ways they are representative of the thousands more which time and space simply don't allow us to cover. This chapter (*Chapter 2*) shares first-hand accounts from mothers whose babies were stolen from them at birth. These stories represent one of the three types of women or typical profiles that were especially targeted to steal babies from by the church and its criminal network-married women who had been previously pregnant and/or were now pregnant with twins. Twin babies were especially coveted to steal and sell as nurses, doctors and nuns could then tell the mother how one twin died but that they were "blessed to still have a surviving baby." (1)

The other victim profiles most frequently targeted, as we shall see in upcoming chapters, were:

1. Single, downtrodden and socially isolated women
2. Young married women from a low socio-economic status and/or uneducated or with very limited, formal education

Now, to briefly put into perspective just how commonplace these cases of baby stealing were in Spain, we should also disclose that the cases and interviews you will read in this book are just a few of the more than 300 interviews that we've conducted since

43

2015. Many were conducted as part of the research leading up to our documentary, with about 50 more conducted during the actual filming. (2)

We've been asked if any patterns have emerged or if there are more female than male victims, where they are mostly from or if they were mostly single or married when victimized.

Well, after the documentary was completed, we went back and tried to summarize some key items about everyone we've talked to before, during and since.

Here's what we found:

Average age of biological parents searching: 75

Average age of adopted babies (now adults) searching: 48

Majority are mothers searching for their biological babies

Minority are adoptees (more women than men searching)

Decade (1970s) when most (currently searching) were stolen

Most recent case that we are directly aware: 2002

When we look back on everyone we've interviewed, still stay in contact with or victims we continue to hear from all over the world with (sadly) stories of new cases, we are most struck with the sameness of what we hear.

It's almost as if those that took part in the criminal network of baby stealing all share the same sort of handbook or manual on how to commit these crimes, these atrocious human rights violations. The same lies, deceptions and methods of operation are repeatedly employed against their victims.

Regardless of time, location, clinic or decade, the "script" would go something like this:

The birthing mother would be heavily drugged, even if she refused, so that her judgment would be impaired. Next, the attending nun or nurse, or both, would begin "prepping" the mother-to-be that it was very "likely" her baby or babies could die due to a variety of reasons. Most frequent of these reasons would

44

be some deficiency or frailty noted by the doctor even before giving birth. Often, the doctor would cite some internal deficiency or condition, so it was harder to contradict by even a close review of the baby. If the woman was married the husband was not permitted to stay overnight with his wife at the hospital nor allowed to be present with her during the birth.

Only rarely was the mother allowed to see, hold or even touch her newborn. The baby was taken immediately to a separate room or incubator out of sight. The usual refrain given was "the baby is too frail to be held and must be quarantined to recover."

When the mother was informed of the sudden "death" of her baby her request to at least see the baby was summarily refused. An exception was in the case of Dr. Vela, a gynecologist accused of stealing hundreds of babies over the past 50 years. His victims tell of how he would show them a dead, frozen baby and pass it off as their newborn before whisking it away. (3)

The final act of this shared "script" was to deploy a caring nun who would comfort the mother and inform her that the hospital would take care of everything so as not to worry. With few or no exceptions we could find, mothers were all told that "you are young and can have more babies."

Meanwhile, family members were given small, sealed boxes and told not to open them as to do so would be a sin. Inside they were told were the remains of the dead baby. They were instructed to immediately take the box to a nearby cemetery and bury it. Only this way, they were told, would the spirit of the baby be blessed. Only later, when they summoned the courage to commit a "sin" against God would they discover the box was either empty or filled with sand.

The "script" even appeared to call for a preferred day and time of the week to commit these crimes. As a former nun who worked at one of the more notorious clinics where baby stealing was rampant, told us, "On Sundays, we were sternly forbidden to go to the second floor where many of the expectant mothers about to give birth were. Except for a few visitors that came in through the side entrances no one else was around. Mothers were informed their babies had died in the early morning hours, usually around 1:00-3:00 am. We all knew what was going on but were afraid to question our superiors." (4)

As one victim, María Consuelo told us, "How ironic it was that on Sunday, the supposed holiest of days was the day my baby was stolen from me. By a nun no less." And as we'll soon see she was far from being the only one.

"Mama, please, quick, take the other baby away before they kill her too."

Paquita was, as she puts it "no shrinking daisy."

As a young, married woman of 27 years about to give birth she had no idea that she was carrying twins. Though her doctor and nurse knew, they kept this detail from her until after the birth. As she recounted the moments just before her delivery to us the memories were vivid and clear as though it all took place just yesterday. In fact, it took place in the year 1962.

Now age 84 with a voice still strong and fully animated, Paquita began, "I went to the doctor's office in Alicante. I had an appointment for a check-up. They assigned me the number 47 but as I took my seat in a small chair in a waiting room I felt a sharp pain in my kidney and another lady who was also waiting in the room said, 'Maybe you are going to give birth right here.' I got up to let the nurse know and my water broke and my mother-in-law who was with me went to tell the doctor and he said, 'What's her number?' and she said, '47,' and he replied 'then she'll come in when her number is called and not a moment before.'

Another woman who was waiting went to her house which was close by and got me towels because I was all wet. Finally,

46

after several minutes my number was called, and I went in to see the doctor. He said, 'That's how I like women, tough.' I was confused, 'tough?' He said, 'Yes, tough not like your mother-in-law who came and (making a mocking voice) was crying, 'doctor, doctor, my daughter-in-law is very sick, her water broke.' He went on, 'No, I like women to be tough like you, not whiney.' After briefly looking at me he then said, 'Fine, the ambulance can take you to the hospital.' I said, 'No,' that I preferred my husband to take me. The doctor then in a gruff manner, simply said, 'Fine, then go.'

Paquita paused in her recounting of her story for us and for our cameras to ask, "Is this what you are interested in? It's not boring is it?"

"Not at all," we replied, "please continue when you are ready."

"Well, when we finally got to the hospital in Alicante, I was brought to a waiting room they had for the 'complainers' and sat there for about 10-15 minutes. Then a nurse came and finally took me to the birthing room. Now, there were 2 or 3 nurses and they laid me down behind a curtain. I couldn't see from my waist down, but I heard the doctor's voice talking to the nurse, whispering so I could barely hear them. But as the first baby was born I clearly heard them say in a regular voice, very casually, as if they had said this many times before, 'What a precious baby girl,' and then a few seconds later when the second baby girl was born they both said, 'What a worthless, ugly girl.'

I was then taken to a room and was only allowed to see the "worthless, ugly baby." The "precious one" was never brought to me to hold or see. María José (her adult daughter) was tiny and was the one I was given at that moment."

As we spoke with Paquita at her home, her second baby, now an adult herself, named María José, shifted in her chair as she

47

watched and listened to her mother share her story to us. Surprised that she was being so open, she also couldn't help but be somewhat amused, "Me, the ugly one is still here!"

Her mother continued.

"They took both babies away from me and told me it was to bathe them. Around midnight or 1:00 am., one of the nurses came to me and said, 'You know, one of your babies, the bigger one is sick.' I was drowsy from the drugs they had given me, even though I did not ask for them, and so it was like she was saying, 'Do you want to go to a parade or something?' I was numb and just a few minutes later, or so it felt, she comes back and now tells me, 'You know, the baby, well, she died. She died just before dawn. We couldn't get in touch with anyone.'

I was alone."

Paquita paused to compose herself and continued once again.

"When my mom came to visit me at 3:00 pm., that same afternoon, she asked to see both of the twin baby girls. I had to tell her that one of them died. She got very upset, almost hysterical and as she was leaving the room, I don't know what made me say this, but I said, 'Mom, be quiet and don't go, please, or they'll kill the other baby too.'

My mother stayed with me until they finally brought us the surviving twin baby girl, the "little, ugly one," my daughter, María José.

They told my husband to go and buy a small, wooden fruit box from a local grocery store so they could place the dead baby girl in the box. The doctor said it was for the fetus. That is what he called my baby. My husband with a very heavy heart did what he was told to do. When he returned with a small box he was told to wait while they took the box and went away from us in another room behind a curtain.

A few minutes later he was given the box, now nailed shut, and told to go immediately to the cemetery which was now closing. 'Go fast, run before it closes and do not open the box, it would be a sin.' As he was leaving, again they called out, 'Do not delay, the gravedigger will be waiting for you to put the baby into a grave.'

He left hurriedly and got into a taxi. He went to the cemetery and they buried the baby girl in the tiny box which they had nailed shut into an unmarked, mass grave."

For years Paquita and her husband suppressed their doubts and suspicions about what happened. Her husband always told Paquita that the whole situation didn't make sense and, after the fact, began to question why they were never allowed to see their baby, alive or dead. But they didn't fully question what happened, the idea was just too crazy. But when other, similar cases began to gain publicity from the efforts of advocates and local television stations began to profile stories of stolen babies, they allowed themselves to think the unthinkable- could it really have happened to them as well?

Along with their surviving daughter, they began to investigate around 2011.

"We discovered that in the hospital where I gave birth there is no evidence or record that I had ever even been there. The hospital officials told us that no medical history exists, it may have been destroyed in a flood around 1982. We checked with the Civil Registry of Alicante. That is where all records of babies born but which do not survive for at least 48 hours are kept. But there they told us no documentation exists before 1978 because everything was misplaced or lost in moving offices from one building to another."

Paquita showed us the birth certificate of the surviving baby, which was recorded largely blank and with irregularities and false information.

She explains:

"Maria Jose's birth certificate (birth record) was left blank. Information about her birth was supposed to have been completed here but was not. It also should have noted that she was a twin, one of two (multiple births) but it did not. A line was drawn through that part indicating that there was not another baby even though there was another born, it was not miscarried. But by making the information for María José disappear and be false it also makes everyone else involved disappear like the name of the doctor and the nurse.

In the burial license there is no name of any doctor signing it even though there must be a name of the doctor. Here, they only inserted my husband's name, Antonio. There was also no burial certificate in this case and by law there must always be one.

She (the cute one) was buried in a mass grave which is normally only for miscarried babies. We had our own private burial insurance and would have buried her in a private grave but did not have that chance."

Paquita's case, which was one of 261 cases that were part of a class action lawsuit filed by Enrique Vila and Antonio Barroso with the State's Attorney's Office (*La Fiscalía General*) in 2011, eventually made its way to a local prosecutor in Alicante.

"So, after over a year of investigation, our case was finally reviewed by this prosecutor who agreed there was a number of irregularities and false records. So, in January of 2012 he ordered a judicial exhumation of the mass grave to confirm her burial site. Following the description and coordinates which my husband provided to the archaeologist, they found the remains of a very damaged and empty grocery box. Around the box were a number of newborn decaying bones. The process of extracting DNA from the bones and testing them took another year. Finally, in 2013, we found that the result of the tests was negative. There was no genetic match between the bones around the empty box and me or my family."

Still dealing with this traumatic news, Paquita and her family received yet another round of bad news. The prosecutor called and informed them that they needed to carry out a second exhumation. The reason, they were told was simply to confirm the finding of the first exhumation.

"Was this normal, standard procedure?"

"Sure," they were told.

Yet, this second exhumation was conducted very differently.

"The attendant at the municipal cemetery who handled our exhumation the first time and had worked there for over 30 years was suddenly fired for no reason. Now, this new guy told us that he (the previous attendant) had excavated in the wrong area. We told him. 'No.' that 'he had followed the exact coordinates given by my husband.'

But the new one ignored us and excavated in an area far outside of where our baby was buried. After 9 days of digging, nothing was found.

Our case was closed (*archivado*) for lack of evidence."

Paquita leaned forward and confided in us that "My husband always blamed himself for not opening that box."

Today, her surviving daughter, María José, continues to keep searching and is a founder and current president of an association of stolen babies of Alicante (*Asociación Víctimas de Alicante*).

She (the daughter) explained to us what was becoming so clear in all of our interviews, that the 'Mafia' would be on the lookout for twins, and that the bigger baby, the one seen as 'cuter or more precious' than the other would be especially coveted.

"This way," she told us, "they would make sure the quality of the 'product' (the baby) was good, and that it wouldn't get sick and die before it could be sold. The smaller or sickly baby would be left with the mother, that way if that one died then it wouldn't ruin their business transaction and profits."

Paquita's husband died never knowing the truth. His last words before dying were, "Paquita, keep looking for the baby. She's still alive."

As Paquita finished sharing her story, Laura, a close friend of her surviving adult daughter, María José, shifted uncomfortably. Hearing Paquita's story brought memories of her own story, her own search for her stolen baby boy, for justice, rushing forward. In truth, her memories, as she confided to us, never stray from her mind. It is like an ache, or a terrible pain that never goes away, and for which, there is no relief.

Still, she wanted the world to know what they did to her and her family. For years she was warned, threatened by officials not to tell anyone. Or else.

"I am not afraid anymore."

Laura Perales began,

"On July 3, 1980 I had a C-section…I had already had a boy 4 years before and they told me they didn't know how I was able to get pregnant again due to a condition I have which doesn't allow for the womb to fully open and makes getting pregnant and delivering nearly impossible. With this condition the bones do not fully open, and there are no labor pains or anything, and the child may suffocate inside.

Needless, to say, I had a lot of trouble delivering my first baby, and with this (the second), they scheduled a caesarean section. This second baby boy, named Javier, I was scheduled to have it done on a Monday, but on a Friday the doctor on duty sees me and tells me that he wanted to go ahead and deliver the baby right then with no warning or notice to me.

So, they took me immediately to the operating room to have a C-section already, that's how it was, they said, there is no need to wait for Monday, and they did it on Friday. Dr. Marín was going to give me a caesarean section, which was the one who was going to see me at the hospital, because I was admitted, he admitted me 20 days before, but on Friday the one on duty did it.

He came to look at me in the morning and said to the nurse 'take her there that I am going to do the caesarean section and I am already on my way'. He asked the nurse, 'has she had breakfast?', and she says, 'no, because they are going to do a blood test,' and he says, 'no need, take her now,' and he did my cesarean section.

Right after it was done, they give me my son to me, and we were taken to the room. My mother-in-law comes, my husband too, and my own mother was already there in the hospital because she was very sick and was dying of stomach cancer. The rest of my family was not able to be there.

My mother-in-law leaves because the next day my sister-in-law was getting married, but my husband stays with me. I give the bottle to my son, I am a breast cancer survivor, I had surgery 16 years before and my mammary glands were removed, and I have no milk and so, I had to give the baby a bottle.

The baby Javier cried a lot. We gave him bottles all day and the next day a nurse enters and says, 'We are going to take the baby to do a test, because since you have had cancer and you are RH- (blood type) we are also going to do more tests.' My husband said, 'Well, I'll wait for them to come back,' and the nurse says: 'No, no, no, you go to court,' but he says 'It's Saturday,' and she tells him 'You must go to register the baby now, but if you want, when you come back, ring the bell and we'll bring you the baby, there is no problem.'

Then my husband goes to the court to try and register the baby, even though it is a Saturday and I am left all alone, and they tell me, 'Look, because he is crying, give your baby the bottle and then we'll take him for a rest.'

I gave him the bottle as fast as I could and they took him away, and they never brought him back.

I never saw my baby Javier again.

When my husband returned he wanted to see the baby and he wasn't there, so, he got very nervous and hit the reception counter with his fist because it was already 5 or 6 in the afternoon and they still had not brought the baby back, since 11:00 in the morning when they had taken him. Then the nurse calls a warden to throw my husband out into the street, and they give him a temporary arrest, (24 hours without being able to enter the hospital).

Later, after he was thrown out he came back with his brother because he wanted to see a pediatrician to ask him where our baby was and why no one would tell him and they caught him and told him 'Look now you'll be 48 hours instead of 24 without being able to return.' My brother-in-law took him to Villena because we lived there, and my mother-in-law stayed with me. As soon as they got home the hospital calls him and tells him that the baby had died. Of course, he came right back, just imagine. Then, when he arrived at the hospital at 12 p.m. he was told that he could not see the baby because it was very purple, and that he must wait until the next day. This naturally made my husband even more angry and he yelled at them and because of that they threw him back into the street and they did not let him come to the room. He stayed at the hospital door all night, and the next day they told him to come up to the room now.

But by this time, it was now 7:00 a.m. in the morning which meant that the staff and workers changed shifts. My husband told one of the new guards that he wanted to see the baby and that he would do whatever it took to see him. The guard told him, 'If you calm down and don't give a show and cool it, we will let you take the baby to be buried, and if not, he stays here for experiments.' They called my baby boy Javier a fetus, but he was 2 almost 3 days old baby, weighting 4 kilos (8.8 pounds).

My husband was crying, it was very bad, and he said, 'I don't want them to keep him for experiments and dismember him.' Then his brother went to the funeral home and bought a coffin, but in the hospital, he was told that he couldn't take him, that the baby had to go straight to the funeral home. They did not give us a death certificate, and then, having no certificate, they forced us to bury him in a mass grave, when we had our private paid-for, gravesite (*nicho*). The doctor never came in to see me or take my stitches out, nothing. After 8 days I was discharged, with a caesarian you must stay 8 days. I had a roommate at the hospital who had a baby girl and she disappeared. They told her that her baby died too. The same day they took my baby boy Javier, they took the baby of my roommate."

Laura continues in a soft but firm manner:

"After the baby is buried, the cemetery tells my husband that they will send him the death certificate in the mail, that is the way it is done. A nurse who I never saw before sent me home. I have a discharge from the nephrologist, because I have a kidney problem since before the child was born and I had that very controlled. But the doctor and nurse who delivered my baby never officially discharged me. They give me a little card, and then said, 'We will send you all the papers, don't worry, we'll take care of everything.'

55

I have had to ask now judicially for them (to get a court order) because I received nothing. Twenty-one years later, my son is called to military service, he was labeled a fugitive.

About seven or eight years ago, I went to the hospital requesting papers because I needed my son's papers and to know what he had died from and they told me that I had not given birth there.

As I am very stubborn and hate being lied to, I went back to the hospital several times. One time I was told that the flood of 1980 destroyed everything. But the fact is there was never a flood here (in Alicante), we have suffered terrible droughts for decades.

One time I went for my records and another woman was next to me asking for records of her baby that was born in 1980. As I stood there, I couldn't believe it but a few minutes later the woman returns with records of this baby being born. Yet, again, I was denied. I got so angry that I went to the police station and denounced them (issued a formal complaint) for lying to me and not giving me my lawful papers. My complaint reached the local court. By chance, the day my complaint was being reviewed there was a demonstration, a protest of many stolen babies at the courthouse door. María José (the adult daughter of Paquita) was there as well. I joined the group, but at the time I really didn't know anything about the stolen babies or how bad it was throughout Spain before meeting them."

At this point, María José, who was sitting next to Laura during our interview, briefly interjected that the protest was one of their first real attempts at making the courts aware of all the cover-ups and none of them knew what to expect.

Laura continues:

"We all asked for our papers (records of the birth of our babies) and finally, Judge Carlos Ferreiros came out to disperse the demonstration. He ordered us to leave but did give many of us a brief audience to hear our complaints. We all talked with him. I explained my case and he told me that he was going to request all the papers on my behalf. Later, he informed me that while he did ask the hospital officials for my records, they told him that 'there was nothing there and that I had not given birth at their hospital, that I had never set foot inside of their hospital.'

When I told the Judge that this was all lies, he said, 'Fine, I will order the grave opened (exhumation).' This was in 2011. As it worked out, my baby's grave was going to be opened the same day as the grave of Paquita's baby.

The actual day of the opening was horrible. No one was prepared to do it. It was done so badly... Carlos (Judge) told me that since it was already 3 in the afternoon, by the time they got to mine, they could not do it that day. María José's exhumation was done very badly, digging for hours and then they found nothing, her father had a very bad time, was very upset.

Judge Carlos said, 'Next week we open yours,' and after three days he spoke informally with another judge over a cup of coffee and told that judge how badly the digging went and that there needs to be another try. The judge asked him whose case it was, and he said it was Laura Perales and she (the second Judge) said, 'Ah, I have her complaint from 2 years ago, I guess we can open it.'

On May 10th they did the second exhumation. My brother-in-law came with me because my husband had passed away recently and they (her husband and brother-in-law) were the two who buried the little box originally.

My brother-in-law described every detail of the coffin, it was beige with round tips, it had a golden edge all around, he gave the Judge all the information. During the dig they found that our box, after so many years of being buried, had shifted down about 1 meter deeper (almost 40 inches). When they discovered and opened it, the box was intact, just as my brother-in-law had described it.

When we opened the box, the coffin, there was an adult's arm inside! That was it.

Immediately, the government archaeologist and Judge ordered the whole area near and around the grave sealed. They put a temporary fence around it, closed it off to the public and ordered all the television media and journalists to leave. They made it a *secreto sumario* (a confidential, secret matter) and told us we couldn't talk to anyone and warned us, 'If you say anything, this is all lost. It will all be made to disappear.' I thought they were going to help me, but I couldn't say anything to the press, or to television, to anyone. Not even other family members.

Antonio Barroso (a lawyer and colleague of Enrique Vila) came from Madrid and they didn't let him in to the cemetery and Enrique Vila came from Valencia and they didn't let him in either and he left. Barroso stayed with another lawyer he brought from Madrid.

Finally, maybe because of the pressure we brought, we were told that the reason for the arm in our box was they used to bury the amputations in a coffin. And they said that 'the nerves in the adult arm ate my baby's bones, that the nerves of the arm had absorbed my baby!'

The government took the arm to be analyzed. The archaeologist and the coroner said, 'We will dig more, because it may be that the arm has remained, but the baby has sunk.' Then they dug more and there was another coffin, and they said, 'The baby must have gotten into it.' They opened the one below and said, 'Oh, there's nothing, we are closing it all up.' They told me that 'Your baby has evaporated.' They looked at each other and said, 'It may be that the earth's movements have misplaced the remains.' Then, they dug further and said, 'Oh here there are bones.' They opened that one, which did have a baby. They opened a total of 5 graves. From 8 in the morning until 4 in the afternoon they dug and opened graves until they were finished.

It was awful, of the five, they only drew remains from two of the graves, three of them were empty. The remains were both of baby girls. But I had a boy. They told me to do a DNA test to prove that neither of the two babies discovered were not mine. But since I had had cancer before I had my son, they figured that maybe my DNA changed, so, because of it, they did the DNA test to my first son.

We waited another 6 months until we heard back from the government. They informed us that while the DNA didn't match the remains of the two baby girls it was still possible that I had cheated on my husband. Can you believe it?

So, they exhumed the remains of my dead husband who had passed away for more than 30 years and removed some bone marrow to do DNA testing. Then, they made me go to Villena to ask for a certificate of good conduct, from the town hall, to certify that I got along well with my husband, that we were a normal family, that I had no problems with my family, that our economy (home finances) were good. They even asked the Bank of Spain for a financial account statement (to show they were not destitute or corrupt). While they collected everything, another year passed. A year after that, I was informed that I must pay a lawyer because the judge cannot read the sentence (outcome of the testing and complaint) without an attorney representing me in court.

The judge told us that the remains were in fact of two baby girls but that he could not continue because his wings had been cut. He said, 'Are you going to appeal?' And my lawyer said, 'Yes.' The judge then said, 'What do I put on the form? Because this is a blatant robbery?'

The judge told us again that to appeal he had to write something, and said 'Well, we can put that there is no money to continue looking for possible remains in the mass grave.' That was what we did. And we appealed to the trial judge. He denied our appeal immediately and he said, 'I am not going to take a case of stolen babies, I will not admit it.' We were also told that my lawyer cannot ask because there is no cause, they would not recognize him as stolen child. There was nothing found for María José either and she was told that her father was confused about the right location of the casket and so they wouldn't keep looking. We are the only ones in Alicante who have done exhumations and there was nothing found. We must be strong no matter what for all the others who have been denied.

While this was all going on, a worker at the cemetery who felt bad for us, told us that 'You are never going to find anything, empty baby caskets are buried here all the time.' When we tried to talk to him a few days later to come to the court we found out he was fired, and no one knew where he lived anymore."

Laura paused to pick up some of her papers and documents she had with her. She began to show us these papers and summarized their content.

"One Judge obtained a document that says that I was discharged from the hospital with my baby boy favorably. Another document here says that my son was operated on because he had lung cancer at birth. Another paper says that for five hours there was no pediatrician to sign the death certificate and because it was late at night it was never signed.

This paper (holds up a paper) says that he died of respiratory problems and was going to have a chest ultrasound, but the machine was broken. I have witnesses, my sisters-in-law, who all came to the hospital and saw the baby and he was fine. They called my sister-in-law to testify and she said that she gave a bottle to the baby on day three at night and he was fine, that is the day they said they operated on the lung. A friend of mine formally declared and said that my baby boy was perfect and that she saw how my sister-in-law gave him the bottle and changed his diaper. That statement from my friend has been 'lost' by the court. The judge told my lawyer, 'Don't ask for more things that I can't give you.' Last year (2017), they called me to court and a different Judge said that he was not going to look at my case until I showed up in court with my supposedly stolen son and a DNA test that proves he is mine. After all these years how am I going to now find him?"

Laura remembered an important detail of her hospital stay.

She continued:

"A woman in San Vicente, who declined to testify because she is afraid of what they will do to her, said she arrived with a pillow around her belly and a million pesetas. I had two hospital rooms under my name, 103 and 107 even though I was only in one. I never changed rooms. This woman came out of the hospital with her birth papers and a newborn baby girl. She was admitted for two days in the hospital with nothing but a pillow! The next day she was discharged and went home with this baby girl whose mother was staying in another room. Now this woman is having a lot of problems with her daughter. She (the baby girl) was registered as being her biological baby. They (the Mafia) told her, 'If you want it (the baby) as a biological one, it is 1 million pesetas, as adopted it is 3,000 euros, half a million pesetas.'

Sometimes I sink down, and I think I can't go on, then, somehow, I recover and keep on going again. For the sake of my baby."

"They called me crazy. But a mother always knows."

Josefa Verdejo, joined on her living room sofa by her daughter, **Mari Feli** and her husband, told us her story, both for

Mara in 2017 and then again for our cameras in the summer of 2018.

"I had given birth to four babies before, each time was perfect, no problems. This last time though I was older (41) and there were complications. I had to stay a lot of the day in bed, I was feeling very sick. I didn't want to eat or drink or do anything. I felt horrible. It was a bad pregnancy. The worst.

Between the seventh and eighth month of the pregnancy I suffered bleeding and had to stay all the time in bed and my doctor ordered me to go to a hospital in Alicante and I was there for 8 days. They then told me I was fine to go home. But only 2 days later, it got worse. More bleeding, pain and nausea. I was rushed to the hospital and by the time I got there I had lost a lot of blood. At the hospital I had to be given a blood transfusion.

The decision was made to have an emergency C-section to deliver the baby. It was actually two baby girls and they were both born alive. The day was November the 6th and the time was 6:00 a.m. One of the twin baby girls weighed 1.850 kilograms and the other weighed 1.600. My whole family was with me and saw both babies. They all said how healthy each looked.

But less than 48 hours later very early in the morning they told my husband that one of my babies had died but not to worry, they would take care of everything, the burial cost, everything.

When my husband and his sister asked to see the baby, because I was too sick at the time, they refused.

He wanted to see our dead baby, and to bury her, but they didn't allow it. We had burial insurance and offered to pay but they said, 'No, it is out of your hands now.' Their excuse was that they already did everything."

Josefa pauses to compose herself and continues.

"I have never gone to bring flowers to the grave, I never even thought about doing it because to me, I knew she was still alive.

Once I got home and felt better I would tell everyone that they took my baby and that she didn't die and everyone said, 'You are crazy, you don't know what you are talking about, That would never happen.'

But to me it is clear, they took the healthier, bigger baby and left the sicker and smaller baby."

[Josefa looks at her daughter and her daughter's husband, slowly leans back on her sofa and reflects for a moment.]

"Later, you start thinking and wonder, how could this happen?

For a long time, we tried to live with the truth, knowing there wasn't anything we could do. No one believed us.

But one day my son saw a girl identical to his sister at a wedding. She was one of the servers. He was frozen, he was staring at her, not knowing what to say or do. Finally, he said, 'You look just like my sister.' One of the waitresses later told us that this girl was adopted, and she told her (the waitress) that her biological mother supposedly died at birth and she was bought by an adoptive father. My son came home and told me, 'Mom you were right all of these years. You aren't crazy.'

I guess mothers can somehow just sense these things.

Since that moment we have been searching, trying to locate this girl. This coming September it will be 15 years looking (as of 2018)."

[Josefa shows us a picture of two young twin girls.]

She explains:

"This is a picture of the surviving baby girl when she was very young, it was taken in front of a mirror, it looks like the twins are together, like they should have been.

We started looking before there were many known cases in the news. We tried to put pictures (of the surviving twin sister) all over and a lot of people would come up to us and say how familiar she looked. In 2004 we did an interview in our local newspaper

63

and then some local TV stations started to call us for interviews, and we did many. We are in the stolen baby association (AVA) and went to many meetings, many rallies but we found nothing.

After 2011 when all those cases were filed (the class action lawsuit filed by Enrique Vila and his colleague) then people started to finally believe that yes, this happened. And maybe, just maybe, I wasn't crazy.

We all hear the same excuses as to why we can't see records or files or documents. The floods ruined them, or it was some fire or rats ate the documents. Lies, all lies."

[At this point Josefa's daughter, Mari Feli shares where they are now as far as searching]

"We all hoped that with the change of government in Spain things would change but sadly, it is still the same. We think a lot of powerful people are involved in this cover-up because otherwise they wouldn't care if we saw our papers, our documents. They would then actually investigate. But they do not.

We will keep fighting but people do get tired. We started strong but now it is a shame, fewer and fewer people attend rallies and fight each time."

Josefa leans forward, "You know my husband's last words were 'María José' which is the name of my stolen baby girl."

"We don't want money. We only want our children. To hug them and let them know they have a family waiting for them with open arms."

Lidia Acebo met with us on the condition that we not disclose the location of the interview. We agreed.

She and several other members of ABRA, a stolen baby association, shared their stories with us. They all brought documents, certificates, papers, licenses and medical and hospital records. The amount of evidence they all had was overwhelming.

64

And yet, each one of their cases was closed or *archivado* for a supposed lack of evidence. How could this be, we wondered?

Lidia, who is the current president of ABRA, explained to us how, by way of also sharing the intimate details of her own story.

"They told me I had a baby boy. I only ever saw the baby in diapers, so we don't know for sure. We know others have been lied to.

He was born at 8 months with no problems. Strong, very healthy. Because he was born prematurely, they baptized him. He was gaining weight. My husband would go see him every day.

I was young, only 16 at the time but I always wanted to be a mother. I would call the hospital every day in the morning at 8:00 a.m. to check in on how my baby was doing. They would always say that he was fine. But one morning after they told me again that he was fine, my husband went that evening to the hospital to see the baby they told him he died the night before, even though they told me he was okay that next morning.

They showed my husband a baby that was very small, not our baby, and he was covered in gauze. You could only see a little of his face which was purple, and the body was very cold.

They told us that they would take care of everything and not to worry about the burial. My husband went to the burial for the both of us. They supposedly buried my son in a mass grave in 1967 even though that, by law, it was supposed to be only for miscarried babies and my baby had lived for several days.

He was very protective of me and didn't want me to suffer even more. When he came home, he told me that the box which the baby was supposedly in was already sealed before he could see the baby inside and that it was very light. Too light. He thought it may have been empty. He was a carpenter by trade and had brought the wooden box to them for our baby.

We always thought they stole our baby boy. We always have had to live with that knowledge.

My children always knew they had a brother born before them, but we didn't tell anyone else. After it first happened, I confided to a neighbor who said, 'Don't say that to anyone. People will think you are crazy and maybe take you away."

So, I never told anyone else for a long, long time.

Years later, my daughter began to watch similar stories of stolen babies across Spain on television and called me up. She said, 'We always believed you but now even more, we know it is true.' My husband said on some of the cases on TV the doctor was showing mothers a dead, frozen baby to trick them. This was just like our case, the baby they showed him had been in a refrigerator.

We started to investigate and to try and collect the documents of the birth and death of our baby. But when we received the documents, they did not make sense. One paper says that the baby died at home, one declares he died in the hospital incubator, another document states that he died in a different hospital and was signed by the same doctor who signed the death certificate from the original hospital. The papers we got from the cemetery states that our baby died in a military hospital. Another paper states he was buried in a different cemetery.

I went to see the Judge, but his secretary told me she would take care of it for me. I showed her all my documents and how they all contradicted each other. After briefly glancing at them, she replied, 'Don't worry, this is not a problem, these are simple mistakes and can be solved.' She hands me a blank form to fill out and says, 'Just tell me the day your baby was born and anything else relevant, the time, what he weighed when he died, all of it and we'll just change the information on the records that are wrong.' I looked at her, couldn't believe what I had just heard and said, 'So, I don't have to look for my son now, I will be given current information?' And she replies, 'Don't look anymore because all the papers will now be correct at least, the case can be closed now.' Again, in disbelief, I replied to her, 'I don't understand, isn't what you want me to do just falsifying official records?' She looks at me for a moment and then says, 'No, of course not, we are just making corrections...we've made a lot of corrections like this over the years.'

I thought, 'My God, all these poor mothers.'

We want to find our children and to tell them the truth. To tell them that we are not crazy. It is sad that these babies, now adults, think their mothers did not want them, abandoned them or died giving birth. They believe whatever stories and lies they were told. We know the truth. In many cases they found out they were adopted when they were much older, many at age 40 or even 50, often after the death of an adoptive parent or both. In some cases, the adoptive parents were lied to as well and really believed the baby they were adopting had been freely given up or abandoned.

But if the parents are still alive, they must tell their adopted child the truth, tell them who they were contacted by, who they paid, how they came to have the baby. Even if it is painful, the adopted children all have the right to know.

We know they have their own life and are all adults now but at least they should know the truth. Many adoptees are frightened to know, to confront a reality that they were told but is not true.

But they all need to realize that they have a family, another family waiting for them with open arms."

To help cope with the pain and loss of her own baby boy stolen at birth, Lidia has over the years assumed more responsibility within the stolen babies of Spain movement. As President of ABRA (a stolen baby association in Sevilla) she helps organize rallies and connects with other associations across Spain.

She shared her motivation and hope which helps keep her going on those days, sometimes weeks, that seem hopeless.

"My motivation." Lidia told us, "is to simply find my son before I die. If I didn't have any hope or didn't still believe it was possible then I wouldn't be here trying.

But it (the struggle) burns you up inside, makes you worry constantly, causes us all a lot of pain and suffering, it eats you up all the time."

Lidia wipes away a tear and steadies herself. She wants us to know something else.

"I try to channel my pain into some creativity. I have written a book about my case and a play. We put the play on locally for the community and high schools. It's to make them aware this happened and to make sure they know we, as mothers, still care for all children. Even those that are not our actual children.

Maybe by chance, my son will come to read my book or see the play and know the truth. I hope, before it is too late."

With the same concern in mind, knowing that time is indeed running out, many stolen babies, now adults, search for their biological parents. Their story and struggle to find the truth starts on the next page in Chapter 3.

Chapter 3
Stolen Babies Who Search

The following are stories that are quite common among the actual stolen babies, now adults, or of siblings of stolen babies. Whether looking for a sister or a brother or for their own biological parents, they all face an all too familiar path of lies, deception, falsified records, and a government either well-meaning but largely impotent or outright hostile to their cause and struggle, depending on which political party happens to hold a majority in Spanish Parliament at the time. Despite holding in their hands overwhelming evidence, they all feel frustration as their cases are closed (*archivado*) by prosecutors who claim their own hands are tied. (1)

Many continue the fight started by a mother or father or both, and now find themselves carrying on the search for the truth alone. Rallies, meetings and stolen baby associations offer solace, support and companionship but there is still a formidable legal and political mountain to climb.

While we've noted before we have been able to conduct some 300+ interviews, there are literally thousands of additional active cases in Spain alone. While time and space does not allow us to even share all of our interviews, below is a sample of what we discovered when we met with either the actual stolen babies or with siblings of the stolen babies. Even in such a small sample size though, the similarities of their stories are astonishing.

"My wife used to joke to me how I must have been adopted. I never dreamed it was actually true."

Vicente Martínez was born in the Valencia Health Clinic on March 14th, 1972. He was officially registered as a biological son to his parents.

Nearly four decades later he learned that this was a lie.

"In 2010 at the age of 38, I learned that I was not the biological child of my parents, not my parents' son.

I was an only child, but we were a normal family, whatever that means, and I never doubted being their son, never heard any comments or saw anything that prompted me to think I was not their son. The physical features are also very similar to those of my parents, we all have brown hair with brown eyes and darker skin, so it did not occur to me that I was not their son.

Why should it?

But, in 2010, I heard a conversation between some neighbors when some cases (stolen baby cases) began to come to light on television. I live in a neighborhood and we have an annual party and by chance I heard a conversation between neighbors who knew me since I was little, and they commented on my name and were talking about the issue of adoptions. They were talking about me, assuming, wrongly, that I knew that I was adopted. This took place in August of that year.

Shortly after, between August until December, those 4 months, I tried to find out the truth on my own. It's funny, my wife always suspected it, she had doubts about things she saw in the family. As a person from outside the family she noticed a cold relationship. When she was my girlfriend, as a joke, she always said 'you must be adopted...it just has to be.'

I never imagined that it was true. During my search, I started asking for documentation without saying anything to anyone. I went to the court, to the town hall, to the parish where they baptized me to see if I was really adopted. In all my documents I appear as their biological son. I do not appear as adopted anywhere. I am, as Enrique says (Enrique Vila) 'a false son,' a son with all the false documentation. (2)

After those 4 months of researching on my own, at Christmas I asked my parents directly if I was adopted. At first they denied it, but after a few days they called me and confessed to me that yes, that I am right, that they could not have children and through a friend who was a priest, and with the help of a nun and a doctor whom they knew, they paid money for me and adopted me.

The priest was a friend of the family, of many years, who came at our home every Christmas to visit, and was close to my parents. So, I went to speak directly with this priest, and he confirmed it to me. He told me that that it was true, I had been adopted and was bought and paid for, but that I should not search any longer. He told me that I had enjoyed a very happy life and my parents loved me very much, and that it was not worth looking for anyone else because I was not going to find anything anyways.

Those were his words. I asked him if he knew who my mother was, but he said he didn't know anything of those details. He simply said that he spoke with a friend he had at the Health Clinic, where I supposedly was born, and that this friend was the Mother Superior (Head Nun) who was in charge of the area of maternity and that he didn't know anything else.

In the end, he told me that he was just the contact for the adoption.

He only shared one more item. And this was that a few weeks after he spoke with his friend the nun, she called my parents from the clinic and told them they had a baby ready to be picked-up.

This seemed to confirm what my parents had told me about the actual adoption. They said that they picked me up as a newborn, and that I was only a couple of hours old at the time. My parents shared with me that they were called very early in the morning by someone at the clinic and were told to hurry to the hospital because a newborn baby was ready to be picked up. At about 7 in the morning my parents showed up at the clinic and

71

were handed a naked baby, me, wrapped only in a blanket and told to come back the next day to collect the necessary paperwork and official documentation. My parents did not ask who the mother was and never wanted to know anything more about the baby's parents or how or why I was available for adoption. They never wanted to know anything more or to investigate. They told me that they were just glad they were able to get a healthy baby.

I found out that I was bought for about 200,000 pesetas (about $4,500 USD at that time)."

We asked Vicente if he had kept pursuing his case officially or unofficially.

"Yes," he told us, "I reported my case with a *fiscalía* (regional prosecutor) but it was closed very quickly. My lawyer Enrique Vila requested all of the documentation from the hospital and that we be provided with the names and information of all of the mothers who gave birth on the date I was born, as with new laws passed in Spain, we, as adopted children, had the right now to such records.

The hospital official did not dispute this right but instead told us that in all of the births prior to 1978 they did not keep any documentation or any record-books, that in addition, everything they did have was destroyed by a fire or a flood. My case then, was closed because the alleged perpetrators had already died (the nun and the doctor at the clinic) and the hospital supposedly had no documentation of my birth or adoption.

Just to get to this point, just to find out this truth took me 7 years of struggle.

During my search, I was also going to the media, appearing on TV and doing interviews for the press.

My parents were very angry because I was looking for my roots. They took it very badly and broke off all relations with me. They disinherited me from their will. They even changed the locks on their house so I could not come in. A year later my mother died and two years after her death, my father died."

With more people searching and more media attention, we asked Vicente if he still had hope that one day, he would find out who his parents really were, maybe even be reunited with them.

"I am still searching. I use social networks and have joined stolen baby associations. I've also had several DNA tests with several possible mothers (about 13 or 14 mothers) that matched the dates of my birth.

So far though, they have all been negative. The tests have been conducted in Spanish laboratories. I've been told by friends though not to trust the labs here in Spain.

Another problem is that I have not been able to get any more clues about my birth because in all the documents I falsely appear as a biological son of my parents.

Whenever I have the chance, I go on TV to see if someone recognizes me or if someone knows something or someone related to me.

I still search but it is hard to keep going."

"I just want to be able to meet my brother and let him know the truth, that he was not abandoned."

In the summer of 2016, we met with **Victoria Utiel** as she shared the story of the ongoing search for her stolen baby brother.

Flanked by her husband Paco, she began:

"My mother went into labor and was rushed to a clinic which was referred to her by her gynecologist who had her change clinics during her pregnancy though she never knew why. He did tell her though that she didn't have to worry about paying as it would all be taken care of as he was sending her. She was given heavy drugs immediately upon her arrival and only remembered waking up and being told she had given birth to a baby boy but that he had died. She was never told what he had supposedly died from.

When my mother was taken to the delivery room, the nuns told my father to stay in the room, but my father ignored them and went down and waited by the door of the delivery room. When my mother gave birth and the nun came out with the child, she saw my father. He told her to show him his son, that he wanted to see him, but she said no, that she was taking him upstairs. My father jerked the sheet in which he was wrapped and saw that he was a boy, that he was pink and was crying. Five hours later they said that the boy had died but gave no reason. The nun told my father that since he had an 8-year-old daughter, he should take her (Victoria) to the delivery room so that when my mother woke up she would see her daughter and could be comforted, knowing that she still at least had another child.

Then I remember that my father came home with my grandmother and they took me to the clinic. I remember entering the delivery room and seeing a nun standing over my mother all in brown.

The nun said to my mother, 'Wake up, your daughter is now here, so cheer up, stop moping.'

My mother told us that although she was nearly asleep, she had heard her newborn baby boy cry. She always believed that they had stolen him. She always believed this to be true. But who was going to think that a doctor and a nun would be so barbaric and cruel?

When the cases of stolen babies began to come out (around 2010), I thought about going to the cemetery where my brother was buried. We always meant to visit him and put flowers there. But, for some reason, we never did."

Victoria pauses and continues.

"In the clinic they told my father that they would take care of the burial and he said, 'No, we have burial insurance and we will bury him.' They told him, 'No, that the hospital takes over the body by law.'

Then, my father reluctantly agreed but wanted them to give him the coffin, that he wanted to bury him and be at the funeral of his son. The nuns kept telling him this was not possible, but he insisted so much they finally agreed. The funeral parlor prepared a sealed, white coffin. The nun said, 'Look Antonio, do not even think about opening the box, because we have done the autopsy and the body is all chopped up, so just remember the baby like when you saw him.'

Now we know that when an autopsy is done the body is not chopped. But at that time, we did not know the process and believed what they told us."

Victoria then shared her efforts to discover the truth as an adult.

"I went to the cemetery to ask for documentation of my brother's burial and plot but to my shock, the cemetery official record-book shows that my mother was single not married which was of course, false, and that my brother was her third child which was also untrue. I requested all the documentation relating to his birth and death but was told there was nothing- no cause of death, no death certificate, no baptismal waters, no records whatsoever. In the cemetery, workers there do not even understand how this can be, as a coffin does seem to be buried with the coordinates we were given, but no official paperwork or documents appear to exist to confirm it."

Later in her search, Victoria held out hope that she was finally going to make progress.

"*La Cigüeña* Clinic was closed in 1983 and I found out that the *Bancaja* (Bank) headquarters that subsidized that clinic had possession of all the archival records. So, I went there with hope, only to be told that in my case, no files or records existed and that somehow my mother has no medical history or files.

Then, I went to court and asked for the official death certificate. They told me that from 1963 to 1972 all documents have disappeared and that they don't know where they are. To this day, I have absolutely no documentation. I reported the case to the prosecutor's office, so that the judicial police could investigate. They took my statement on February 8th and on the 28th of the same month they closed my case. They told me that there was simply no documentation or records, and that any errors I may have found were perfectly normal at that time and they would not investigate anything.

My brother was born on the 2nd and just two days later he was already supposedly buried. I figured out that the 4th the year he was born fell on a Sunday and on Sundays there are never any burials permitted in Spain, anywhere. I also went to Alboraya Street (the location of the mother's clinic) and they don't have any records on my mother ever being there either. When I asked them the names of the doctors who worked there during that year, they told me that they have no way of knowing."

After a moment to compose herself, Victoria continued on.

"It is clear, that they are hiding the information and my brother is still alive. I have no doubt my brother is alive. My mother was robbed of her baby. After 4 years in this fight, we are in the same position as when we started. We have not achieved anything. We are desperate. We attend rallies every month, we talk to the political parties, but we are always told the same thing, that there is no budget to create any national DNA testing labs or to conduct exhumations or to do much of anything for us.

We are really desperate.

I just want to be able to meet my brother one day and let him know the truth, that he was not abandoned, that we mourn his being stolen from us, his real family. I feel the need to meet him before it's too late and that's why I'm in this fight."

In the summer of 2018, we returned to Valencia to once again talk with Victoria, her husband Paco and their daughter, Victoria. Sadly, Victoria, the mother, had, in the interim, passed away from her struggle with cancer. We sat down with Paco, flanked on one side with their daughter and the other with their beloved family dog, Lolo, and they were gracious enough to let us film them as they updated us on their search. What follows is a brief synopsis of this conversation. Paco, who is looking for a stolen baby twin sister, recalled how he and his wife Victoria used to try and keep each other motivated so neither would give up looking. He and their daughter vowed to keep looking for Victoria's brother to honor her memory.

"We will never stop looking for Victoria's brother.
And I will keep looking for my own twin sister."
In **Francisco Rocafull's (Paco)** words:
"We were both born at home and were both very healthy babies. About 6 months later, my twin sister got sick and my mother took her to the Sanjurjo hospital in Valencia, because there were no pediatricians in Paterna where we lived at that time.

After just a brief time at the hospital, the nun in charge there tells my mother that the baby has died of contagious meningitis and they tell her to bring the other twin (me), who no doubt had the same sickness and was also going to die. My mother came home right away to check on me and saw that I was fine and didn't take me to the hospital. My parents were not even allowed to see the baby's body and the next day the hospital buried her in a cemetery that did not belong to us, even though, we had paid for

77

death insurance with a different, private cemetery. The nun at the hospital told my family they were required by law to take care of the burial.

Years later, I filed a formal complaint with the police and was informed that they found my death certificate in that hospital, mine! I never even went to the same hospital where my twin sister supposedly died so soon after being admitted but somehow, my death certificate was formally registered and signed by the nun and a doctor. In fact, the death certificate of mine and that of my sister were signed by this doctor who did not even start working at that hospital until 14 years after the supposed death of my sister. How is that even possible?"

Paco held Lolo, their pet Yorkshire Terrier closer in his arms, leaned forward and told us that this case got even stranger.

"You see, my sister has not one, not two, but three different official dates of her death. In the family book it says she died at 1 year and 2 months old, but the hospital has two different dates. In 1972 someone asked the hospital for all our information related to this case, who asked for it? I have no idea. But I know that no one in my family asked for it.

We always had doubts about the death of my twin sister. None of the official papers matched with what my mother knew to be true, about her birth and her alleged death.

When the complaints about stolen babies were filed by ANADIR in 2011 with Enrique (Vila) as the lawyer of record, that was when we also decided to file a formal complaint. The more papers we asked for and were able to review, well, the more mistakes we found. After investigating, Enrique believes that the reason I have a death certificate with my name on it is because the hospital planned to steal me. As you know, they really wanted twin babies, those could be separated and sold easier. (3)

What he believes happened was the certificate was already made and the parents who paid for my sister illegally, simply took my sister because they could choose if they wanted a boy or a girl. In the cemetery there is nothing about her burial. She was supposedly buried in a mass grave, which they didn't have to bury her there because my parents had burial insurance and in Spain, these mass graves were supposed to be for miscarried babies and my sister was not, she was over 6 months old.

When I went to the cemetery with the coordinates given to me by officials at the town hall, the cemetery worker told me that such coordinates did not exist. They informed me that there was nobody buried at the coordinates on record. How is that possible?"

Paco touches his daughter Victoria on the shoulder, and they repeat their promise to keep on searching, both for his twin sister and for her (Victoria, the mother) brother.

"You know, for years, we were bringing flowers to an empty place. Praying to a hole in the ground that was empty.

Our cases have been closed, and all the false information I have shared with you is all blamed simply on 'honest mistakes.' They tell us that nothing can be done. Prosecutors tell us they will not investigate and that our cases are closed due to lack of evidence, period.

What are they afraid of? Why do they not want us to find out the truth?

We don't want money. We just want to know where our loved ones are and that they are safe."

"The nuns told my mother to just shut-up during the delivery and stop complaining because for sure when she was conceiving the baby she wasn't complaining."

Eva Páramos is searching for her brother born September 19, 1972 in San Sebastián, Spain.

79

Eva was born with spina bifida, the most serious type of this disorder. Here, the spinal cord and the meninges (tissues covering the spinal cord) protrude from the back. Eva has endured more than 20 operations and while confined to a wheelchair, she continues the fight to find her brother. (4)

We spoke with Eva in early 2020 to hear, in her words, her struggle and what happened to her mother during birth.

"I was born after him in 1974. And that's when my mother started to really doubt things because the first birth was attended by nuns who were kind of nurses, and when I was born, she told them she didn't want to be attended by nuns again. When I was being born, in the delivery room, they told her that I was coming out with problems and that was when my mom´s alarms went off because if the first one supposedly had problems, why didn't they say anything to her? My mother says she was drugged and hardly remembers anything. The documents from the hospital say that they heavily sedated her in the first birth, which was the birth of my stolen baby brother.

He was born in the former residence of our Lady of Aránzazu, which is the current Donostia Hospital. I was born in the same place and the medical team was the same in both births. Both the doctor and the nun who treated her are dead now, I have not been able to talk to anyone. My father was not allowed to see the baby, nor any other relatives who were there. From what I can tell, he had to threaten people there just to see his baby son, but they did not let him. They said they took care of the burial and everything, that it was too late to see the baby and they already buried him in a mass grave.

When my mother was taken to her hospital room after the delivery, she was told that the baby had died, that he was strangled by the umbilical cord. My mother barely remembers as she was still drowsy from the drugs that they gave her, and the official papers claim the baby died due to being born macerated or too thin and wasted away to survive. This was not what they told my father.

My mother was treated very badly, was told to forget it and to go get pregnant again. They teased and mocked her. When she was in the delivery room, they told her to stop complaining that for sure when she was doing it (conceiving the baby) she did not protest. The nuns were very mean and treated her very poorly.

There is no death certificate. I have gone to the bishopric (diocese) to see if he was registered, because the family book has the seal of the bishopric as he was born and was registered in the civil registry, but this does not show his name. But I do not understand. If, he was born dead, why is he registered in the civil registry? And who went to register him? But when we ask for documents at the registry office there is nothing, nor are there documents of baptism or relief waters. There is nothing in the cemetery either.

Since I was a child, I always heard my mother saying that my brother's birth was very strange, that something happened, that my brother is somewhere. She also could not spend time searching because she was always with me in hospitals, I had 2 operations within 2 months of my early life. After seeing Antonio Barroso on television with stolen babies cases, and hearing cases almost identical to ours, I got in touch with Antonio, with ANADIR, but since they were in Madrid and we are in San Sebastián and it is quite far, and difficult for me to travel, my case didn't move forward.

One day as I visited a town square in San Sebastián, I saw many people gathered and asking for signatures with a sign that read "stolen babies" and I approached and it was the association (San Sebastian Stolen Baby Association). I signed their list and told them my case, and we started investigating and asking for papers, and nothing matches in my records. It appears to be all lies and stuff they made-up.

The hospital papers of my brother's birth, where it is supposed to say the name of the baby's father, well, they kept that part blank. My father's name is not there, I think they wanted to make her (the mother) seem like she was a single mother so they could justify taking the baby away, claiming she was single and unfit to raise a baby on her own. I also asked for the hospital papers of my own birth and there is everything, my father's name, my mother's, even what my father did for a job and his workplace address.

When we put together all the papers, we filed the complaint, but it was closed immediately by the *fiscalía* (prosecutor). My mother went to put the complaint, but they barely asked any questions, as if they didn´t care and they closed her case and never even bothered to notify us. As the months went by and they did not call us, I called them, and they told us that they had closed it a long time ago."

We asked Eva if she had tried to do any DNA tests to see if there was an existing match with her brother.

"I did DNA tests in *Neodiagnostica* (A Spanish based DNA lab) with no positive results. We think that their DNA result is not valid though, and the analysis is wrong. In June (2019) I did more DNA tests with the United States labs like *23andMe* and *MyHeritage*. We will see.

We have had all the doors slammed in our face. This is now our last and only hope."

"In 2008, when I had my baby daughter, I realized how much my mother must have suffered having her baby stolen, and I decided then to start investigating."

Chary Herrera González is the current President of the SOS Stolen Babies of Cádiz, Spain. During the filming of the documentary, we met Chary in Cádiz and she shared the story of her mother and that moment when she decided to devote herself to carry on the search for her stolen baby sister.

"When I was 15 my father told me to be very alert just in case I saw a girl a year older than me who looked a lot like me, but that she would have a brown spot on her leg. I was so confused, because I didn't know anything about a sister, all I have are brothers.

He said 'Your sister was stolen in the hospital. When you are older, look for her. It will cost you a lot of money and hard work, because there must be important people involved in a cover-up.'

My father then told me that on January 10th, 1975, my mother gave birth to a girl in the hospital. Two nurses were constantly saying they were going to show her around because she was very pretty, but we don't know to whom they showed her. The night after she was born, the nurse took the baby for the night to keep with all the other babies, and in the morning, they told my mom her baby became suddenly very ill but they didn't let my mother go see her baby. When my dad arrives, he goes to see their baby girl and the nurse and nun tell him that he can't see her because she just died. My dad insisted on seeing her and to avoid a major scene they finally showed him a closed package of gauze and adhesive tape from a distance and told him that they could not open it because she was prepared for burial, but not to worry, that they would take care of everything.

My mom had been isolated all this time in a room by herself, but shortly after telling my father, they moved her to a different room with a woman that had just given birth. My dad kept asking when the burial was going to happen, but they wouldn't give him any information. Then, when they left the hospital, they weren't given any records or papers. My parents always thought the baby was stolen by the doctors because she was so pretty. The doctor told her to get pregnant right away to cover the pain from the baby's death. I was born a year later. After he told me the story, I would look around for girls like me and would ask them if they had a brown spot on their leg. I know it must sound silly, but I was desperate to find my sister.

In 2008, when I had my own baby daughter, I realized how much my mother must have suffered losing her baby and decided to start investigating. I discovered that the records and documentation were full of lies and gaps. The hospital records said the baby was born at 7 months and was not fully developed, when, in reality, she was born full term and was beautiful, healthy and strong. It also had two different causes of death, one was respiratory failure due to being premature, and the other was macerated which means it died inside the mother before birth due to being shriveled or emaciated. All lies.

I denounced the facts in court in 2010, and my case was the first stolen baby case in Cádiz. I started looking for other cases like mine with Facebook and the internet and many people started to contact me, so I created the SOS stolen baby association. The prosecutor's office saw signs or evidence of crimes from my complaint and filed my case with a Cádiz judge, but my case, like that of many others, was closed for prescription (statute of limitations). They said I should have filed earlier but how can anyone file a case before they know or have evidence of such a crime? If you file prematurely then you can get fined and jailed for falsely denouncing someone or a hospital.

But I did not give up and kept trying to get an exhumation. Now, along with 45 other families, we have been authorized to do exhumations. We are finding out the babies were not buried as their families were told and, as it states on their official documents. So, it is very possible, even probable, that these stolen babies, now adults, are alive. We even found 4 empty coffins, and 5 other babies are not in the graves where they were supposedly buried. We are proving they stole babies. In my case, they found a body with a little bracelet, and we are now waiting for the DNA results. But it is difficult as we don't trust the DNA labs here in Spain.

Unfortunately, my father died last year without ever knowing the truth about his baby.

Maybe someday the truth will come out."

"The same day my father died, I saw her…in the hospital hallway, it was her, I mean, it had to be her, same look, same face, same hands, same hair as my mother…everything."

During the summer of 2018, we traveled across Spain conducting on-camera interviews and attending stolen baby rallies and meetings. One of our stops was in Sevilla, Spain. We met a number of stolen babies attending a rally there organized by the *Asociación Sevilla Bebés Robados*, to hear their stories and see their approach in trying to raise awareness for their cause. **Ñoñi Torres**, who travelled to the rally from San Fernando, a small town on the coast of Cádiz, was eager to sit down with us and to share her story which had an unexpected twist.

"On September 11th, 1967, my mother had a set of twin babies. My mother was barely able to see them, though she remembered them as both strong and healthy. But no matter, the nun at the hospital told her that both of them died. They gave no reason but said they would take care of everything and not to worry.

For a long time, my mother, myself and our family have been gathering the facts and collecting evidence. We were able to get an exhumation ordered this past April (2018) but all of the tiny boxes (coffins) had dissipated and you could see that they had been filled with sand. There were 47 boxes found during the exhumation and all of them were totally empty. We were told several different stories as to why, but one official said that 'No, the real reason is all of the previous coffins were transferred to another cemetery.' That too, turned out to be a lie. My mother was told her babies were buried in a certain wall or section in this cemetery but when that turned out to be false then we were told they were buried in a mass grave, but when that was searched there was nothing there either.

We have a lot of proof based on the evidence, records and papers that her babies were stolen and that signatures on death certificates were falsified, including them signing my father's name on these certificates which he didn't do and this was not his signature.

Even the cause of death is weird. No real cause is given though it does show that my mother was injected with heavy drugs normally used for farm animals to speed up their delivery, even though it was used on her with no reason given."

We asked Ñoñi if she and her mother were actively searching for her babies and Ñoñi's siblings. Her answer was startling.

"Well, I've located my sister (!)

I mean, it has to be her. The same day my father died, I saw her…in the hospital hallway, it was her, I mean, it had to be her, same look, same face, same hands, same hair as my mother…everything.

She doesn't know who I am…yet. I have been following her on and off for quite a while now. She is identical to my mom. From my own research, this girl has 4 different birth dates. I doubt she has any idea that she is adopted.

I've told my mom of this girl and I took her where this girl works, and she saw her from a distance. But she got overwhelmed, nervous and emotional and we had to leave. It is her, no doubt.

I don't know if I'll ever get the courage to meet her and tell her.

It is a scary thing. Who knows how she will react?"

How would any of us react?

Now that we have met several mothers that are searching for their babies and several babies, now adults, who are searching for their biological parents and family, we'd like to close this chapter with an astonishing story from the point of view of both the mother and of the long-lost daughter.

"They ripped my baby girl from my arms and gave her to a couple who took her back to Mexico. For years they tricked me into thinking the wrong man had taken my baby. But now I know the truth."

Mercedes (*Merche*) **Moya Martín** had a healthy, baby girl on May 7th, 1978, ironically enough, on Mother's Day.

In 2019, now with the benefit of being able to look back on her life's events with insight, Mercedes shared her story with us.

"I got pregnant in 1977. I came to Madrid running away from my daughter's father because he was involved with drugs. I did not want that life for my daughter. I went to work at the home of some journalists who, upon learning that I was pregnant, sought an association in Carabanchel that was managed by a well-known nun, Sister Pura."

Along with Sister María Gómez Valbuena, who was later indicted on crimes related to illegal adoptions and fraud and Dr. Eduardo Vela, who worked closely with her and he too, was indicted and actually went on trial for similar charges, Sister Pura was alleged to have engaged in baby trafficking for decades. She oversaw and managed a number of "baby chalets," homes where single, often impoverished mothers stayed as they neared their delivery dates and once they gave birth, were often discarded once they were coerced into signing away their rights of parenthood of their newly born babies. Mercedes stayed at one of these chalets under the management of Sister Pura.

"They did the amniotic fluid test and I was told everything was fine. I began to realize that many of the mothers like me left without their babies. I told Sister Pura that I wanted to keep my daughter, because I was working and could support myself and my baby. I already had a child who was staying with my parents. I was single but had means to be a caring mother.

But she ignored my plea. On May 7th, Mother's Day, against my will, they induced me to deliver my baby 15 days before it was time. I had my baby at the Francisco Franco hospital. She was healthy and they gave her to me to breastfeed. All seemed to be fine. The next day, Monday, a worker from the court came to register newborn babies and I registered my newborn baby girl. I filled out her birth certificate as María José Moya Martí. Talking about it now I still get nervous.

The following day, on the 9th, Sister Pura came to my room and told me to put on a little dress that we were leaving. I said, 'No, I need to be here for 3 more days to recover and besides, I have not been discharged.' She said, 'You'll see how fast we go when I say we go.' She left for a moment and returned with some papers and we left. There was a taxicab waiting for us at the hospital door. I soon realized this was the same taxicab that was used to separate mothers from babies. The car made a surprise stop at a photobooth. Sister Pura was next to the driver in the front and I was in the back with my daughter. The nun gets out and says that she is going to take a picture with the baby girl that looked very pretty. At that moment I panicked, I grabbed my daughter and I didn't want to give it to her, but as my daughter started crying, I let her go. I wanted to get out and run after her, but the taxi driver shoved me back into the car and drove away while the Nun was still holding my baby.

We went to *Tu Casa* (the Chalets run by Sister Pura) and when I got inside, I ran to the bathroom crying. The door opened and there stood Sister Pura. I asked her where my daughter was, because I assumed, she would have my baby with her. She told me that I was a whore, an insignificant low-class whore, and that I would never see my daughter again. Then I told her that I was going to report her to the police, and she said that if I went to the police, she would have me thrown in jail. I swear I thought they could do it. I was only 20 years old, from a small town and had nothing, and I was completely alone. She was spitting insults at me for 4 days and said she would not feed me until I signed the paper waiving all rights to my baby. We went to a place where she said there was a notary, and I was told I had no choice, I had to sign.

At that moment, I couldn't even think straight. Sister Pura had given me some pills to help with post-partum nausea, but they only made me dizzy and unable to focus. I felt like I was flying, I don't know what she gave me, but I vaguely recall signing something.

I always thought my baby was sold to Manolo Escobar (a famous Spanish singer) because other nuns told me he had my baby now and because I saw him at this notary public place that same day. For forty years I believed this lie. Now I know this is not the truth.

Then Sister Pura took me to *Tu Casa* and while I was packing everything to leave, she grabbed my arm and gave me an envelope. I took it thinking that it had the hospital papers, but when I looked at it, it had money. I threw it at the nun and told her that I had not sold my daughter. She snatched up the envelope and laughed at me and I left."

Mercedes shared with us her pain and the emptiness she felt for years, always wondering where her daughter might be and if she'd ever get to see her again.

"About 9 years ago (2009) I found out that someone was searching for me. I was able to contact this person and I discovered it was my biological daughter. She was a little reluctant to let anyone know we connected with each other because her adoptive parents were still alive. I told her that I didn't want to be hidden, I wanted to say that I had found my daughter for everyone to know.

What I now know is that when her adoptive parents arrived in Mexico, they registered my baby as their biological daughter. They had to bring witnesses and everything, but they did. María José (the daughter of Mercedes) has told me that the adoptive parents were sending Sister Pura money every year for many years, until she died.

As for María José, initially, our relationship was complicated. I felt hurt that she wanted my identity as her real mother to be hidden. For quite a while, we didn't really talk which only deepened my feelings of regret and pain.

In August 2018, I asked my daughter to take a DNA test to remove any lingering doubts or concerns she may have had about our connection. She told me that she had no money and I told her that I would pay. I paid it, and I went to a laboratory (LabGenetics) in Spain where I had previously been tested. They took María José's DNA sample and told me that it was negative, that there was no match between us. I couldn't believe this result. I took the print-out of my results to a fellow stolen babies fighter, Paco Rocafull, who reviewed the results with a special DNA analysis computer program he has at home. He told me there was indeed a positive match, a 99.999% match. "Absolutely, no doubt," he told me.

I went back to this lab and re-did the DNA test. And again, they told me it was negative. I told them they were not just wrong, but it was clear they were deceiving me on purpose. Two weeks later, I did it again and it turned negative again. Then I sent them the study that Paco did and then they have felt so caught that they have quickly said that there must have been mistakes made and they were sorry. All lies, there was no honest mistake, it was a hoax to cover-up the truth. Now I have a lawyer, Guillermo Peña, and we are suing this laboratory for intentional fraud and will go to trial if need be. I have already spent over 10,000 euros on my case, including private detectives, and I am not a wealthy woman."

María José Ramírez González was born on Mother's Day, 1978. Shortly after we spoke with Mercedes, we were able to then get her daughter's (María José) story.

In her words,

"My adoptive parents had tried and failed several times before to have their own children. My mother had suffered miscarriages, the last one was when she was pregnant with 6-month-old twin girls. Her doctor told them they should adopt because if they continued like this my mother could die. They wanted to adopt here in Mexico, but since they were not married by the church because it was my father's second marriage, the church did not allow it. The church refused to send a baby into a home they viewed as sinful. Before she died, my mother told me that they had seen a beautiful boy, about 6 years old, in an orphanage and they had fallen in love with that child, but they were not allowed to adopt him because they were not married by the church.

My adoptive dad was an airplane pilot, he was a captain with the Aero Mexico Airline. He told me that he had a friend who was always very lucky and had bought a lottery ticket and gave one ticket to my dad, one to my mom and one to my Godmother who is my mother's sister, and they won! So, they all went to Spain with some of the prize money because my parents loved Spain. They went to bull fighting rings and toured everywhere with my Godparents. My Godfather who passed on a few years ago, was a psychiatrist. In Madrid they met a friend of my Godfather's who

91

studied with him at UNAM (*Universidad Nacional Autónoma de México*) and was married to a midwife from a place called *Tu Casa*.

This midwife told my parents that she could help them get a baby there through Sister Pura. They were told that the babies were from mothers who did not want their babies or who could not keep them. They arranged with the nun (Pura) to take a baby but this one died so the nun told my parents to pay for all the hospital and burial expenses of the dead baby and then she would get another. That is why, my parents always told me 'we didn't pay for you' because technically, they paid for the other baby. They took me out of Spain with a Spanish passport as María José Moya Martín and when they arrived in Mexico, a court there told them that because I was their adoptive daughter they could not change either my original name or nationality until I turned 18. With this my dad was very worried and said no, people are very cruel, because the Mexico of that time was very conservative and a baby had to be natural, the fruit of marriage and not adopted. He said, 'I did not bring this girl here to suffer, to be mocked, no.' He also believed that I would love him less if I knew I was adopted."

What María José shared next was rare even for illegal or improper adoptions.

"My adoptive parents got rid of all the Spanish papers and records of my birth and adoption. They burned it all but a piece of paper that had the name of the hospital, the mother's name (Mercedes), and little else. Then they registered me as if I was born in Mexico and I was their own biological daughter. They then re-named me María José Ramírez González. There were 2 witnesses, and at that time you did not need hospital papers, or a doctor who said you were born there, you just needed to present yourself with two witnesses who said you were born there. Their word was accepted.

Later, when I was 14 years old, I found out I was adopted. My mom told me, and then my dad made a fuss because he didn't want to tell me. But I told him that I loved him the same. It was a surprise for me to find out, although I always wondered who I looked like. My mom was very tall, very white with small honey-colored eyes and was very thin. My dad was brown-eyed and brown-haired. My mom would tell me 'you look like your grandmother.' Since my Dad's mom was the only grandma I met and she had white hair and blue eyes, well, I believed it, but I noticed that other things did not fit well together about my supposed background.

But I really didn't miss anything as I was their only child, their princess. It was a big blow when they died, my mom 10 years ago and my dad 6 years ago. I didn't tell them that I was searching because I didn't want to hurt their feelings but after their passing, I was able to search more openly. When my mother died, I really felt the need to know my story, where I came from. When I found Mercedes, my dad was still alive and he felt sad that I was searching and so, I stopped communicating with Mercedes for a while. When he died, I felt I was not harming anyone for searching. My parents always thought that everything was legal and that my biological mother gave me away so that I could have a better life because she couldn't take care of me. My mother had encouraged me to search, so if I could find my biological mother, I could give her peace, I could tell her what a happy life I had with my adoptive family. About 8 years ago I contacted a stolen baby association in Spain and gave them all the information that I had and told them that I was looking for my mother, and on Facebook we met, because she had been also searching for me.

Mercedes was very happy and wanted to tell everyone, but I had many reservations because my father was still alive. Then I started to block the photos she posted on my wall, and she felt very hurt. Of course, I didn't understand the bad situation she had experienced, because I was stolen from her, she didn't give me away. She remembers the pregnancy, childbirth, how they ripped me out of her arms ... and I don't remember anything, I just lived with my parents in Mexico. I was very surprised because my goal in knowing her was simply to thank her for giving me up for adoption and for telling me a little about my story and why she gave me up. I did not intend for a close relationship. She got very angry, wished me well and said goodbye. Over the years, she wrote to me and asked me to do the DNA test. My dad was already dead, and she told me the whole story of how everything happened and how she had searched for me since they took me. I saw online all the interviews she had done while looking for me and I learned about stolen babies from Spain. Finally, I understood much more.

My parents will always be my parents, but I also want to meet my biological mother and have a relationship with her. I still haven't been able to meet her in person, but I would like it very much. Now I don't have the means to go to Spain because my two daughters also want to go to meet her and it would be a big expense, but they are very excited to meet their new grandmother."

In the next chapter, Chapter 4, you will hear the strange but compelling case of **Ascensión López**, a stolen baby, who may just wind up in jail for, as she claims, simply telling the truth about who helped steal her.

Chapter 4
The Strange Case of Ascensión López
Clara Reinosa, A Girl Betrayed

As we were setting up to interview Ascensión López as part of our documentary film, she was going through her own personal papers from a variety of folders. Every few moments she would pull a piece of paper or a document or even an official certificate and show us off-camera. Always with a question, How, she would ask, can anyone not see the truth? How could anyone deny what happened to me as a baby and what is happening to me now, as an adult, and as a mother of my own daughter?

How indeed?

As we talked with Ascensión and reviewed more and more evidence she selected from her bulky, personal files, it became even more astonishing of the position she found herself in currently.

Accused and convicted of committing the crime of *calumnia* against a well-known nun, similar but not exactly like the civil crime of slander or libel in America, Ascensión sat with us in an apartment not her own, in a location she asked us not to divulge. She conceded that she was also low on funds and unable to work due to poor health and facing a possible jail sentence unless she paid a hefty fine which she could not afford to pay. (1)

All of this, Ascensión says, is due to the simple yet profound fact, that she got up and told the truth on national TV in Spain. She stated how she had been stolen and who coordinated the theft and sale of her as a baby. She held up her evidence in front of the cameras and soon after she found herself in the crosshairs of a powerful nun and an even more powerful church.

The fact that the nun in question was her own aunt simply made it strange but certainly, based on the evidence she compiled, no less believable.

Ascensión also told us that, apparently on advice of her lawyer, she could not actually say the name of her aunt, the nun, as being responsible for her (Ascensión) being stolen and sold as a baby. We assured her that we would not ask her to do any such thing.

On the other hand, we are under no such advice or court order. So, when you do see the aunt/nun's actual name in parenthesis below it is our doing not Ascensión's.

But we're getting a bit ahead of ourselves here, aren't we?

Soon, our cameras were ready and so was Ascensión.

"I was born in Sevilla, Spain, but I was raised in Almería. It was a normal life, I guess, it is true that my parents were older than most of my friends' parents. People would joke that my parents were more like my grandparents and at the time it was funny to me, but I never thought anything more of it.

But my life totally changed and took a turn for the worse when I was 8 years old though. My daddy got very sick and one day when I came home from school, I found out that he had just died. When I came into our house there were a lot of people, some I knew, many I did not. I heard someone say that the girl should not find out. I started to panic, and despite being told to not go, I ran to my daddy's bedroom and I saw that he had just died. He wasn't even cold yet when I reached out to touch him, I ran from his room and went into my room and threw myself on my bed and started to cry. I remember crying and then looking up as a member of my own family (her aunt, the nun Dolores Baena) came in brusquely and asked very harshly, 'Why are you crying, you silly girl? That man wasn't even your real father. He bought you when you were born. Stop crying.'

So, that was how I found out that I was a stolen baby and that this man who I knew as my father since I could remember was not my real father."

Ascensión pauses as she looks intently at a slip of paper from her file. She pulls it out, holds it up to the camera and briefly provides some context.

"See, according to this record, I already was given the birth name of Ascensión on May the 7th but just 2 days earlier in the *Casa Cuna*, I had the name Consuelo (she holds up another paper). And then, just 2 days later, on the 9th of May, the records show that I already had been given the name López which was the name of my adoptive parents. How is that possible?"

Continuing, Ascensión selects more documents from her file to show us.

"See this letter? This is a letter with her signature (Baena), this is her name and her signature, and this is where she writes the president of the governmental council of Sevilla thanking him for his interest in the baby, me. And here (pointing to a note) is where she (Dolores) served as a witness to the adoption, instead of there being any name of an adopting parent it is her name only as the primary contact person. How could she not have known?"

A few moments later, Ascensión continues her personal narrative.

"At the time I have a lack of memory from the point when my daddy, my adoptive father, died. I don't how long time passes but I know I changed, I became very quiet and I was always sad."

We ask Ascensión if she talked to her mother about her feelings, about her loss of her father and her being depressed.

Her answer comes slow and with much emotion.

"No, before my daddy died, he was very sick and for about 3 months having to stay mostly in bed. And during that time some things, some terrible things happened to me by members of my

97

own family. And after they happened, my family members, male members, would tell me that 'You are bad. And if your father ever finds out how bad you are it would kill him.'

Ascension takes a moment and continues with what is clearly a painful recollection.

"I can't say exactly but just imagine a little girl of 8 years alone with two adult men who force her to do things. Sexual things. So, when my father died all I could think of was it was my fault he died because I did bad things and he found out and it killed him.

I have never talked about this before. It has taken me 50 years just to verbalize what happened to me."

Ascensión takes a few moments to regain her focus and we encourage her to continue her story but only if she is able and willing. She tells us she feels the need to set the record straight.

"Some years go by and my mother one day comes to me and says that 'I found out you had doubts about who you are and maybe even you know we are not your real parents. It is true. It's time you knew the truth.' Then she proceeds to tell me.

To fully understand we need to travel back in time a bit to Franco and the Fascist regime. My father was a military trained man, a dictatorial person. He was very close to the Francoist regime. He had a high position in the *Falange* (Franco's feared, coercive guards) and my mother was a typical woman of those times, submissive and born and raised to obey her husband and to serve the regime.

So, she tells me that one day she is home and the phone rings, and it is my aunt (Baena) and she tells my mother 'Come to Sevilla, there is one almost done here.' When my father gets home my mother asked him about the call, what did it mean? and he told her that they are going to go to Sevilla to a place and to adopt. He doesn't know if it will be a boy or a girl. This is how my mother found out they were going to adopt a baby. She told me she never had the intention or desire or even the need to be a mother. She said she went along because it was my father's desire and she was obligated to obey her husband.

She told me they stayed in Sevilla about a week waiting to get the word that the baby had been delivered and was ready to be taken. She cried the whole week because she never wanted to be a mother or adopt a baby. At the time she was already 60 years old. She had no desire to be a mother at 20, so just imagine how terrible she felt forty years later.

It was at that moment when my mother was telling me all of this that I felt the need to know what really happened and who were my real parents. And when I started to ask for more details, my mother would always tell me the same version while other members of my family would tell me different stories, different facts.

My intuition or instinct, whatever you want to call it, was telling me that someone was lying to me. And whenever I would see anyone in my family and ask them about it, I would get a different version, and no one would give me the straight answer. But the only consistent thing they would say was that my father's niece, my aunt (Baena) who lived in Sevilla knew all the details. But anytime I would ask her (Baena) directly, she would tell me, 'Look all you want, you'll never find her (my real mother).'

But time passed and in 2011, when the subject of stolen babies came up more and more in the media and on television in Spain, I started to get in contact with stolen baby associations and ask for my documentation. I saw my documents, my papers (Ascensión gestures to her file that is on her lap) were the same as many of the cases of stolen babies on television. Misinformation, forged signatures, dates and names that don't match. Lies.

In Almería, the small town where I lived, well, I figured my case would be the only one. I thought about maybe starting a stolen baby association of Almería because I really, just wanted to investigate my case. But I soon learned there were many cases just like mine. I was stunned. As more and more people heard of me and the association idea they came forward. Not too long after there were over 300 cases that I knew of that were similar.

Meanwhile, I contacted my aunt, the nun, and said, 'Look, I have asked you many times in the past to tell me what really happened to me. I asked when I was a girl, when I was an adolescent and now, I am asking as an adult. If you are honest then I won't file my case and make all my details public. Just tell me the truth and I won't go further.'

I just wanted to know who I really am. I wasn't looking to cause trouble.

And she says to me, 'Do whatever you want, look wherever you want, you will never find out anything, you'll never know the truth.'

And that was when the stolen baby association of Almería was born. Enough was enough."

We asked Ascensión to tell us how her search for the truth had gone, what had she found.

"I have been searching now for years. Still, there is missing information. I am always looking for more clues but like so many of us victims, often, because they close our cases or lie to us or destroy records or hide the records in church archives, there is only the media or films like yours to help get the truth out.

In my case, not too long ago I was asked to come to a TV show in Spain and tell my story. So, I did. I told them how my records show I have 3 identities. Until the age of 14 I grew up believing my name was María Dolores. In the official last will and testament of my father, my name is stated as María Dolores. But when I was age 14 and I went to get my DNI (national ID card), I requested my birth certificate in Sevilla and there was no one listed under my name as existing. I told my aunt, the nun, and out of nowhere, she says, 'Go ahead and try the name Ascensión.' I tried again, this time using the name Ascensión and soon after I was sent my birth certificate. And nowhere on the certificate does it say I was adopted. Time passes a bit and I get the courage up to ask more questions and this time, I ask for my adoption file. And to my surprise I receive a file and in it my name is stated as Consuelo.

So, this is why I speak of 3 legal identities for me, one person. All public documents with the same last name, same names of my parents, everything else the same. And every time on these different records appears the name of my aunt and her signature, as a witness and the person who processes my adoption. If I say too much more who knows, maybe they will penalize me more.

My mother told me that a lot of money was paid for me. On the TV show I didn't accuse her (Baena) of stealing me or making money off of the sale of me as a baby or anything. I just said, 'Look, this is what the documents show.' Nothing else."

We wanted to clarify the charges which Ascensión faces at this point. So, we asked Ascensión if, during the TV show what she thought got her in trouble was simply reading the name on the documents which was the name of her aunt, the nun.

"Yes, right after the TV show aired, she (the aunt) files a criminal complaint of *calumnia* (insult and slander, doing damage to someone's reputation) against me and the court accepts the complaint and finds me guilty. I am convicted and am ordered to pay a fine of more than 55,000 euros (over $60,000 USD) to her as compensation for being insulted and if I don't pay it then I go to prison. My health is poor, I am staying here at a friend's apartment and I have no job. I am destitute.

101

I am scared now to even talk to her or have friends talk to her, she is well-connected, powerful, she was awarded a medal by Queen Sofía for her service to the church. I am afraid of what else she will have done to me or punish me for trying to tell the truth. Some people, other victims have tried to talk to her and ask her to forgive me. But she just tells them I got what I deserve. But what do I deserve other than just the truth? Just knowing who I really am before I die?

If, nothing else, I am doing DNA testing because I am ill and want to know what hereditary illnesses I have so my daughter can know and be tested. If I had known before, I could have prevented things, now my life is shortened and the quality of what I have left is diminished.

It is hard not to conclude she (the aunt) knew a lot about the adoption since she signed all the papers and admitted that her uncle (my father) wanted a girl so she requested a girl (those were her words). She is the one who wrote up the application and got all the documentation, how can she not know something?"

We discussed with Ascensión some of the particulars about her court sentence. If, she cannot pay, the time she would spend in jail would come to about 6 months.

"If, the nun (Baena) forgives me then the case can be dismissed. But she says she will never forgive me. I guess as a nun that is her idea of Christian charity. But again, I ask, what did I do that needs forgiveness?"

After talking with Ascensión, we interviewed her lawyer at the time, Juan de Dios, at a stolen baby rally in Sevilla. He told us that Ascensión accused her aunt, Dolores Baena, without actual, direct proof and went on to praise the professionalism and honesty of the law enforcement officials, the court and the judge who presided at her trial. One of our film crew thought we might have filmed the prosecutor of the case by mistake. No error. We filmed the right guy. Let's just say he was more respectful of the opposition than any defense lawyer we ever knew of in the US.

He did hint of a possible "bombshell" in her case which, to our knowledge, never materialized.

We did hear from several other sources who wished to stay anonymous for fear of reprisal that the "bombshell" is that Dolores Baena is really the biological mother of Ascensión. We cannot either confirm or completely eliminate this as a possibility. We can share only that Ascensión has promised to one day write her memoirs and once the fear of being jailed more or fined more is gone, she says all the facts will finally come out.

Until or if, that day comes, we can only wish Ascensión all the best. Which we did.

In the next section, Clara shares her own dramatic story.

Clara Alfonsa Reinosa: A Young Girl Betrayed.

"Justice doesn't function for people like us.
It only protects the wealthy and the corrupt." -
Manuel, Clara's husband

We had heard quite a lot about Clara even before we sat down with her in 2018 to talk. How she had gone public with her accusations of her baby being stolen and how she had pointed an accusing finger at several people, including, at the time, the Minister of Defense for all of Spain, Margarita Robles. (2) Some within the stolen baby association community depicted the woman we would soon be interviewing as a determined yet nearly out of control woman, hell-bent on getting justice.

In person, at least with us, she was anything but as described. Firm yet self-contained, passionate yet introspective, deeply reflective on all that had happened to her these past decades.

"I got pregnant when I was young, very young. It was a delicate situation. My home life was complicated, very abusive. We were nine kids. One time I came home, and my father was drunk, and he beat me. I didn't know where else to turn so I went to the social worker that was handling my family's case. That same day I shared with her what happened, she saw the situation at home and took me in her car to a center for single mothers and mothers-to-be in Barcelona, called *Santa Eulalia*, it was run by nuns.

Shortly after King's Day (January 6th, on this day Spain celebrates the Three Kings and kids receive presents), around the 11th or 12th of January until May the 10th I stayed at this Center. I was happy. I was with other pregnant women and children and I experienced what clean sheets were and had 3 meals a day. I felt like I had escaped the situation at home. I was more optimistic. I also got healthier. I didn't receive any doctor visits during my time there.

On May 10th, I was taken by car by a woman, I know now this woman was Teresa Cervelló (a lawyer), anyways, she takes me from *Santa Eulalia* to a building called *Casa de la Jove* in Barcelona and she told me that I would start regular doctor check-ups, that the medical center (to have the baby delivered) was closer from here (*Casa de la Jove*). This was untrue, where I was staying before was much closer. The very first day I arrived at *Casa de la Jove*, I was told to hurry up and get ready, shower and pack as fast as I could that they were taking me to the medical center. A different woman, Cristina Rimbau, tells me she has been assigned to be my social worker, takes me to this other medical center. I have since discovered that this too, was a lie, as she only pretended to be a social worker and ended up adopting my baby without my knowledge or consent. I was under the legal guardianship of the juvenile court and my assigned judge was Margarita Robles.

When I arrive at the medical center, they conduct several tests and I am pleased because they told me everything is fine, the baby is strong, and I heard its heartbeat by ultra-sound. They told me it was a baby boy. At this point, I am a little over 7 months pregnant. I was told I was at a public medical center. I know now that this was also false, it was then and still is today, a prestigious private medical clinic. I was only 14 years old at the time. On June 2nd of that same year, I turned 15. On June 18th, they gave me a blue blanket, since I was pregnant with a boy I was told, and a few other baby items, some diapers, some pacifiers, things like that. I was told by one of the nuns to get ready, that it was time to deliver, that everyone was waiting, but I had no labor pains or anything and I wasn't due for another 2-3 weeks.

I did as I was told though and got ready. They called a taxi, not an ambulance, which I thought was very strange. I got in the taxi and they gave me some pills to take as I was very nervous. I took them and a few moments later blacked out because I don't remember anything else, not getting into the clinic, not delivering my baby, nothing. I only remember waking up and being told I gave birth. My baby was born at around 4-4:30 a.m. I was informed. I asked to see and hold my baby, but the doctor told me that things went badly, and my baby boy had died during birth.

I was in shock. My mind went blank. I was numb. I couldn't even cry or scream.

It didn't feel real. I asked what happened and all they said was the baby was small and didn't survive. Then, I did start to cry, and the doctor said, 'Stop crying, you are young, you can have plenty more babies.' I felt all alone and just remember wanting to see and hold my baby. Then she left and I was literally all alone except for my pain.

I stayed in the clinic for 2, almost 3 days, and during that time, no one visited. My family was under state guardianship and weren't allowed to come. The people like Teresa Cervelló or Rimbau who held my hand leading up to my delivery never visited or checked on me once I had given birth. Every once in a while, a nurse came to check my blood pressure, she would see me crying but would say nothing, only that I was making too much noise for the other patients.

Besides the emptiness, I felt very bad, I wanted to run away. But I couldn't even walk. I wanted to leave but they wouldn't let me go out of my room. Finally, on the 21st of June, I was discharged and the director of the other center, Mercedes, picked me up and I told her that my baby had died. She didn't seem surprised at all and said the same as the nun, 'You are young, you can have more.' When I told her how terrible it was to not see my son or hold him or touch him, she just told me to put it out of my mind, forget it, that I can have more babies, to stop crying.

On the way back to the Center, I told Mercedes that I had 17 stitches from the pregnancy and was still bleeding a lot. But when we arrived, she told me that I needed to go and couldn't stay there any longer. I remember saying, 'But, Mercedes, where do I go? I don't have anywhere to go. I am bleeding, I can't walk, I'm scared.' And she told me, 'You need to call someone because you can't be here.' I begged her to let me stay just a few days. The official records show that *Casa de la Jove* discharged me on the 21st of June just a few days after I left the hospital. I didn't know or understand my rights or what being under legal guardianship meant. It was never explained to me.

I may have passed out though, because I was put in a small bed and given antibiotics as I had a very high fever. Mercedes and a nun both told me that as soon as I could walk, I needed to leave.

A short while later I put some things in a small bag and left.

I remember walking to the Barcelona train station and wandering around and crying.

I walked close to the train tracks and decided I would jump in front of the next train that came and end everything. The pain, the loss of my son, all the memories of abuse.

But as a train was approaching, a man was on the platform, walking his dog and saw me crying. He told me that things would get better, to not give up, that life really was wonderful. Those words stayed with me and I decided not to jump."

Clara pauses to show us some of her documents. She has stacks of documents and many files. It appears she has as much or more "hard evidence" than any of the victims we had previously met with as they shared their stories. We promised to film these documents and learn more after her story.

She continued:

"Manuel (now, her husband) and his mate had promised to pick me up at the station. But they didn't show. I was sure they had also lied and deceived me. I thought that I was a fool for not jumping. Just at that moment, I heard my name, it was Manuel and his mate, Angela. They took me to an apartment not too far from the station and let me stay there to recover. They traveled on to Germany. For 6 months I stayed there alone. I didn't know how to cook, so I ended up eating a lot of *bocadillos* (sandwiches). I spent Christmas alone. I would see mothers with their babies and feel very sad and depressed.

Manuel returned but not with his partner, Angela. They had broken-up. He took me to a psychologist to try and deal with the loss of my baby boy. He was struggling with this divorce and was unable to see his children. We bonded over our shared sorrows. Over time, we got close. Years later, we married and have been together since."

At this point, Manuel comes into the room and promises to return, as he has some things that he too, wants to share. Clara laughs a bit, saying how between the two of them he is the one even more angry at everything. She returns to her story.

"In 2013, I got a phone call and was told that they have some news for me, but it would be best if I was not alone. Manuel was with me, so I told them to go ahead. I started to get very nervous. The man asked me if I gave birth on June 18th, 1987 and I said yes and asked him why he was asking these questions of me. He told me that I had given birth to a baby girl not a boy, that they had lied to me and that this baby girl, now an adult, my daughter, was looking for me and wanted to meet me in person.

I thought it was a joke, a cruel and sick joke. I told them how I had a baby boy and he died. The lawyer said, 'No, we have uncovered the truth, we have the actual records. You had a baby girl. She is alive and wants to see you.'

I fainted.

When I woke up, Manuel asked me what had happened? I told him. He called the number back and it was Eduard Hernández, a psychologist. Mr. Hernández explained everything the same to Manuel. We wanted to see him in his office, but it was Friday. We had to wait until the next Monday. Can you imagine the weekend I had, not knowing if this was true or not?

Monday finally came and we saw Mr. Hernández. He gave me all the details, when I gave birth, the day, time, the clinic, the attending doctor, everything. I was convinced and said, 'I want to see my daughter.'

The Friday of that same week we had an encounter (reunion)."

Clara briefly showed us a photo album which was given to her by her daughter, then continued.

"My daughter, named Marina was already in the office, waiting for me to arrive for our encounter. Though we had never met before, she told me when she saw me from the window, she knew it was me, her mother. As for me, I could feel that it was her, my daughter.

When we saw each other in person we both started crying, like little children, we couldn't stop crying. We didn't want to let our hands go from each other. Physically, Marina is very similar to my own girls (Clara and Manuel have two girls with each other). She gave me a photo album she put together from the time she was born until the day of our encounter.

She explained to me that she had been looking for her biological parents since 2012. She wrote to the clinic and the doctor asking for her true biological origins. She wrote to the clinic and the doctor who attended to me and asked for my name, but they had my name on the forms incorrect. The date of birth was changed, everything. Her (adopted) father bought Marina as a baby for 6,000 euros a month for a year. Marina always knew she was adopted.

At the beginning, everything was wonderful. We got along wonderfully. I had her baptized at Santa Susana, we talked, we travelled together. She helped me with the formal judicial complaint for my case and gave me copies of a lot of the paperwork she had been given. Her adopted father knew she was looking for her real parents, but her mother did not, she had no idea. They would tell her Marina was with friends or at school, anything but the truth because they knew she would not approve.

Why is that? It is because she is not a legitimate adoptive mother. She is Cristina Rimbau, the woman who pretended to be my social worker and told me she would care for me was the one who took my baby from the clinic without documentation. Just 36 hours later she had the baby inscribed and later filed for a provisional admission and claimed the baby was abandoned by the mother, all the while she knew of course, I was the mother and had my baby taken away from me by her. She took the law in her own hands and she is not the only one who conspired to do this, not the only one to blame.

Margarita Robles, the judge who was my legal guardian, and was supposed to protect me lied and falsified public documents, and knew what had happened to me, my baby and why. I am constantly asking her for an explanation, I don't care that she is powerful and believes herself to be beyond reproach, she needs to answer for what she did as well. She falsified documents with my identity to facilitate this illegal adoption. She knew my family was under state tutelage for domestic abuse, sexual abuse to minors and abandonment but not even 2 months after I gave birth she falsified a document to say I was 17 and could be tossed into the street with nothing, no protection or care. No, I had just turned 15 when she did this. I couldn't get a legal job or even a national Spanish ID. I was still a minor and she swore that I was of legal age and no longer had to be cared for by the state.

Who authorized them to give me the pills that drugged me, so I had no recollection of the delivery or birth? Who else could it have been but her?

I asked her to explain why she did this to me, why she had my baby stolen, why she violated my rights? She said she did everything in the best interest of the minor, that I should leave her alone and never talk to her again.

I just want an explanation as to why she stole my rights as a minor, a mother, a woman, why?

I want my dignity back, to say she made a terrible mistake, to admit what she did was inhumane and to tell me she was sorry.

The judge (in her case) believes I knew they were taking my baby and that I authorized it. I did not, and if I had, where is the signed document, where is my consent? Lies.

The real testimony of a victim in Spain in these cases is worthless. I will keep saying the truth, and it is that in Spain it is legal to steal another mother's baby, especially if you are connected to powerful people. I get calls and am told by government people to stop making a 'social alarm' and to be quiet. I am telling the truth. It is not my fault if it is unpleasant for them to hear the truth. They stole my baby, not a car, or a toy, or a thing, but my baby. I will never stop fighting."

We asked Clara what she thought was behind all of these illegal adoptions, the baby stealing in Spain.

"At the root now is money and corruption. The ones behind this evil are just waiting for those of us involved as victims to die, to simply go away. They want Dr. Vela to die so the truth doesn't come out, old victims who have searched for their babies for decades to die with their false documents and their memories.

What happened to Ascen (Ascensión López) is shameful but they are punishing her because she didn't follow the formal process that they wanted her to follow. But why would she file a case? Why? Only to have it (*archivado*) closed despite all the evidence she had collected?

In my case, I am not scared of what will happen to me. If I am lying then Cristina Rimbau, denounce me. If I am lying, Teresa Cervelló, denounce me. And if I am lying, Margarita Robles, denounce me, if you dare.

I have received threats from anonymous callers who told me I had better stop talking about Margarita Robles that I had my baby stolen, and I had better watch my step or maybe the same happens to my other children. I reported all of this to the police. Nothing was done.

I am not scared.

I will not stop until they admit the truth of what they did. They stole my baby and covered it up."

Stolen Babies of Spain- Valencia

Paqui

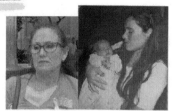

María Jesús

Valencia Rally Group 2018

Paco & Lolo

Enrique with father/Enrique with son

Ralliers signing petition

Nun at rally

Gigante costume

SBOS victim

Rafael

Antonio at the rally

Stolen Babies of Spain - Alicante and Cádiz

Chary

Paquita

Josefa's "twins"

Mari Feli and Josefa

Margarita and Jesús

Ángel

Soledad

Laura

Cádiz Exhumation

Alicante Sunrise

Cádiz Sunset

Stolen Babies of Spain- Sevilla

Esmerelda and Gracia

Manuela

Ñoñi and Mara

Lidia and Carmen A.

Conchi and her daughter

Carmen F.

Alfonso

Lidia

Church in Sevilla

Sevilla by Horse and Carriage

Stolen Babies of Spain - Ascen, Clara, Raquel, and Magaly

Ascensión

Clara

Ascensión - Public Accusation

Margarita Robles

Manuel

Raquel

Magaly

Baby Raquel's Announcement

Magaly on radio

Puerto Rican TV

Panama City, Florida

Old San Juan, Puerto Rico

Stolen Babies of Spain - Inés Madrigal

Little Inés

Inés with her Mother

Inés with her Father

Inés and Mara, the interview

"El Rey"

Stolen Babies of Spain - The Trial of Dr. Vela

"¡Justicia por fin!"

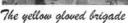

The yellow gloved brigade

Inés in court

Inés facing the media

Dr. Vela in court

Tony, María José and Matilde

Inés walking to her supporters after Day 1 of the trial

Protesters surround Dr. Vela as he exits the trial

Stolen Babies of Spain-Málaga

SBOS Málaga Association

Encarna

Lourdes and family   Málaga Beach

Isabel Assoc. President

Stolen Babies of Spain-Bilbao, San Sebastián

SBOS Bilbao Association

Mara and Isabel, Bilbao

Andone in San Sebastián Cemetery

Guggenheim, Bilbao

Leti and Marga

San Sebastián

Stolen Babies of Spain - Barcelona

SBOS Assoc. of Barcelona

Dolores age 93, and Adelina

Gaudi's Lagarto

Oscar and Montse

Joan being filmed

Barcelona Street Artist

"Would Jesus steal babies?"

La Sagrada Familia

A meeting of the SBOS Barcelona Assoc.

Stolen Babies of Spain - Experts and Activists

Francisco González de Tena

María José Esteso

Enrique, Mara, in Madrid

Pablo Rosser

Soledad and Mara

Carmen del Mazo

Chapter 5
Enrique Vila, His Story
Reunited? Julia and Susan

We met with Enrique Vila in-person during the summer of 2018 and since then have been in close contact as evidenced, in part, through our professional collaboration with Mr. Vila in the development of this book. Since 2018, Enrique has continued to work as an advocate on behalf of victims and recently, became the first lawyer to present a stolen baby case from Spain in front of the United Nations Committee on the Rights of the Child in Geneva. Enrique was also there at the start. As we chronicled in the documentary film, he and Mr. Barroso were the first to file a class action lawsuit in Spain in 2011 on behalf of over 260 stolen baby victims. From that point onward, the issue began to receive more media attention, domestically and internationally. Shortly thereafter, members of the European Parliament, responding to a number of formal petitions by victims, also sent committee representatives to conduct investigations and offer recommendations to be implemented by Spanish officials to address the claims of victims. We will examine this aspect more closely in Chapter 10. (1)

But, as Enrique makes clear in his interview with us, and in our follow-up discussions, there are powerful factions and institutions within Spain like the Catholic Church and leaders who want this issue and its victims to simply go away. Many are political descendants of Francoism, and continue to do everything from flatly denying there even is or ever was a problem of stolen baby victims in Spain, denouncing them and advocates like Enrique as "fakers" or using their power to throw obstacles in the way of victims at every step to ensure the truth stays buried.

Enrique asserts that some in the media who speak on behalf of the entrenched powers that simply want this problem to go away or victims to die off, also accuse victims and advocates like Enrique of just looking for publicity and money. Though, as Enrique also makes clear, he and stolen baby victims across Spain have no interest in getting money for their pain, their loss and their suffering. They and he though, do want to get at the truth, once and for all.

For over 30 years now, Enrique has been working on behalf of victims, whether they were stolen outright as babies or had adoption papers falsely inscribed as being born to the adoptive parents (not actual biological parents) or the place of birth falsified or both. Enrique shared that what keeps him going are the encounters. Those instances when he is able to help facilitate a reunion between family members is, by far, as he puts it, "The best part of his job. Those moments are truly fantastic."

Before we look closely at a few cases from his legal files, which he has generously chosen to share with our readers, we first wanted to share with you his own story. Though, he has been an advocate for stolen baby victims in Spain throughout his professional career, he first felt the pain and shock of finding out he was not who he thought he was, at the age of 24 years old.

In his own words:

"I didn't know I was adopted. I was adopted as a baby. No one in my family, and they all knew, ever said anything to me. I studied law in Valencia, when I was age 24, my adopted father got lung cancer and had to stay in the hospital for quite some time. His cancer spread and his ability to reason or think clearly greatly deteriorated. One night I was at home by myself, organizing his papers and documents because we knew the end was near. And there, among the stacks of papers I found an old adoption letter. I was shocked!

Here, I was already dealing with my father dying and then I discovered he wasn't my real father. It was for me, a brutal shock. The first thing I did was to look at myself in the mirror and I wondered out loud, 'Who am I, really?' I was searching for my own identity in my reflection, searching for who this person in the mirror was when something strange happened. A memory of my childhood came rushing back to me. When I was 8 years old, I was playing with my cousins and they were teasing me, telling me that they didn't love me because I was found on the street, not really family. I started to cry but somehow, I managed to compartmentalize and suppress this memory for many years. Not anymore.

But like I said, since I was now a lawyer, maybe it was the perfect storm in that I was adopted because it drove me to investigate and try to discover the truth. I wanted, needed to know who my biological parents were and started to look into my own case. Soon, I discovered many problems with my documents, my records and what was being told to me. I learned not only how to check into my own case and the records where I was born at the *Casa Cuna Santa Isabel* in Valencia, I also began learning of many other similar cases with similarly false and fraudulent documents and records. Little by little, people began to call me to see if I could help them. I contacted an organization founded by Paco Lobatón, called ANDAS, which was helping people find their loved ones, to aid in investigations. I decided to help them and so I became their secretary. During this time, I learned even more about the best tactics to find the truth in these cases, and in my own, to have the best chances to find my biological mother. Eventually, I began to specialize in this area and devote my practice and career to helping stolen baby victims.

Early on, in 2009 when my first book on the subject (stolen babies) came out in Spain, I started to become known as the adopted lawyer who was helping victims like himself find out the truth. Later, Dr. Vela would mock me by saying on TV that everything was a lie and I was just some lawyer who made up the idea of stolen babies to sell books...I am so happy he will finally face trial in the Inés Madrigal case.

The truth, of course is, that here in Spain, justice, if it functions at all, it functions very slow and inconsistently."

Enrique shared with us a very detailed explanation of how there is not a national, judicial consensus on how best to address stolen baby cases and that, depending on what part of Spain you live in, local judges and prosecutors have sole discretion. The result is very few cases are aggressively investigated and prosecuted. The national courts, as Enrique asserts, have little to no interest in getting to the bottom or in pressuring or making prosecutors do more than just a superficial, hasty investigation which ends in cases being closed (*archivado*).

"Victims and their families across Spain are discouraged. The burden on getting all of the proof rests on the victims. They must essentially, conduct the investigation, find all of the evidence, put the case file together and bring it to the prosecutor. And even when they have the time, money and resources to somehow do this on their own, the prosecutor almost always simply closes the case immediately, citing lack of evidence or claiming too much time has elapsed for an investigation to be launched."

From an American perspective, where prosecutors tend to be very aggressive, even zealous, we found this hard to believe but not shocking, from what we discovered in the past 3 years of research. We asked Enrique though, given all of what we know, still, why do so many prosecutors seem to run from the evidence being brough to their offices in these stolen baby cases?

"Well, a clear example of why more is not done is illustrated by my own case. In 1988, no adopted person had the legal right to look for their biological mothers and to be provided with records and documents from where they were born and cared for to get the names of their parents. But in 1999, the government at the time changed this law and granted all adoptees this right.

So, after this new law was passed, I legally demanded that the nuns from where I was born give me the name of my biological mother. They refused. I filed a lawsuit against them as they were in clear violation of this new law. My case was dismissed in record time with no reason given to me as to why. But I know the real reason why. The president of the attending audience (like a judicial hearing or panel) is a prominent member of Opus Dei. These people are like a cult and have tremendous power in Spain and do everything they can to protect the Catholic Church and keep their dirty secrets hidden at all costs. (2)

So many illegal and improper adoptions have been made in Spain for decades now and who profited? Who was paid millions of Euros? The church.

It has been a mafia of baby stealing and buying.

So, where has all the money gone? Of course, they know.

That is why the church in Spain does not speak out like in other churches in other countries with similar problems like the UK or Ireland. Here, the church, closely aligned with the Vatican have no desire to help victims. They could open adoption records and give comfort, aid and the truth to thousands of victims and help thousands of families reunite. But they refuse. Because if they did it would prove what we all know anyways, that the church conspired with and closely worked with Franco and then with profiteering doctors, nurses and social workers to steal babies, forge and falsify records and hide these records to keep their own guilt hidden.

We don't want any of their dirty money. We want only the truth. I want only to find my mother before it is too late."

[Enrique has written and published a book called *Lettere Di Un Bastardo Al Papa* (Italian, 2018) [Letters From a Bastard to the Pope], where he calls on the Pope to release these hidden records and passionately implores him and the Catholic Church to help not hinder the ongoing search of victims. He actually had a brief meeting with the Pope in 2019 and gave him a copy of his book personally. To date, he has not heard from the Pope or any of his emissaries]. (3)

As we began to wrap up our lengthy though, very informative session with Enrique at his residence in Spain, he shared a final thought about his own search.

"Before it wasn't so overwhelming but now, after turning 50, I feel time is running out...my mother must be at least 70 by now and who knows how long we both have left to reunite?

Time keeps passing by and it is cruel to think we will never find each other.

I've experienced some dark days. It is satisfying to help others, but it is hard to think that I may die without ever meeting or getting to hold my mother.

All the cases I work with are unfair. But for me, it's like a heart doctor who dies from a heart attack.

Maybe, one day my kids will find my biological family. Even after my death, the race will continue. I just won't be around to feel that moment."

The following are from the case files of Enrique. They illustrate the illegal methods of adoption which prevailed for many decades in Spain and those who facilitated such "improper or illegal" adoptions and profited off of the desperation, poverty or the socially difficult circumstances which young mothers found themselves in during the strict and morally rigid Franco regime.

One of the challenges in these type of cases is that while the law does provide adoptees to find out the name and identity of his or her biological parent(s), due to the false or fraudulent "inscription" on the baby's birth certificate, putting down the names of the adopting parents as the biological parents, it can make it very difficult for the truth to be discovered. This is so, whether the law is on the side of the adopted person looking or not.

In compiling this book, we asked Enrique to share any cases from his files which held a special place in his heart. He welcomed the opportunity to do so. Below and in the following chapter are four such cases with names slightly altered to protect privacy:

Reunited? Julia G and Susan.

Julia was born in Spain, half Spanish and half Anglo-Saxon ancestry. She had been searching for her biological mother and had conducted several DNA tests, including, the USA based laboratory, *23andMe*.

Briefly, the following is the synopsis of Julia's case, as told to Enrique by Julia during his interview of her as a client and his work on her behalf.

"Who am I?"

"This question has been in my mind for 32 long years, and it has caused me many days and nights, thinking how to perform my search to find some clue.

However, in my case and by accident, I discovered in my childhood and after a discussion with my family, that I was not the daughter of my adoptive parents. That the names I had so proudly carried were not those of my blood. The surprise was brutal. It was a blow to me, and I felt it deep inside of me and through my body and soul. It shook me and made me want to desperately find out my true identity, an identity that was hidden until one day of my adolescence, which already seems so far away.

I was born in Gerona, Spain, on August 19, 1967. As soon as I learned of the surprising news, I went to the civil registry of that city, and found out that I really was adopted. On the actual birth certificate, they did not put the name or information of my biological mother. It did clearly state though, the specifics of my adoption and my adoptive parents' names and their marriage and marriage license information.

I was overcome with questions. It is hard to explain to anyone not adopted why it is so very important to find out who your parents are, and to know of your true biological ancestry and origins. Many take this for granted, naturally. They have no doubt and accept their origins for what they are, good or bad.

Since the discovery I was adopted, I guess my journey for the truth began.

In Spain, the right to know the biological origins of the adopted ones was not recognized until 1999. My first few years of inquiries were in vain. Even the Law did not support me. My adoptive parents did not tell me anything. My father refused to cooperate or to tell me anything only to promise me that the truth of my origins would remain a secret, that he would take it to the grave with him. (4)

I wondered of course, if everything was legal, why would he act this way?

I was able to find out from the hospital where I was born and discovered that I had been in an orphanage for a few months before my adoption. But this new information had not given me any clue as to the identity of my biological mother.

More questions came to my mind. Was I the 'fruit' of a relationship of love? Was I born out of someone being raped? Maybe from some fleeting sexual encounter? Did my mother give me up voluntarily or was she coerced into it, deceived, maybe never even knowing her baby was still alive?

During my search, my adoptive mother began suffering from senile dementia, so she was unable to help me much even if she had wanted to help. She only told me that I was very ugly at birth, and that my biological mother was possibly a foreigner (I am blonde with blue eyes and white skin, something not very common in Spain) and that information offered me a clue but to what? Or where?

My adoptive father, once my mother died, even tried to complicate my search further, or justify his fatherhood, telling me a ridiculous story in which I was his biological daughter, the result of an extramarital relationship that he had with a Belgian girl, apparently on some business trip. I did not believe this at all and through investigation it has been proven to be just that, a lie.

Over the years I searched on social networks, using social media and tried to reach out to possible relatives or anyone with information related to my case that could help me. But it was mostly frustrating. In 2011, as you know (Enrique Vila and Antonio Barroso), a collective complaint was lodged with the Spanish Prosecutor's Office, which alleged that for decades a very broad and expansive network existed which stole babies in Spain, sold them both in and out of Spain and falsified adoption records and documents to cover-up these crimes, existed. A mafia. This news, which was covered in Spanish media, only increased my desire to continue to search, since I could be a stolen child, and therefore perhaps my biological mother did not want to give me up.

I dived even more into social networks, in stolen baby associations, I asked and researched without rest. I even did the DNA test with a girl from Valencia, who thought we could be sisters because of the coincidence of dates, but the result was negative.

In 2018, I made use of a mediation service that had been set up in Spain for adoptees who wanted to find their roots, through the *Diputación de Aragón*, which in turn contacted the *Generalitat of Catalonia* on my behalf for certain records and information. They never responded.

I also contacted a university professor from Gerona, who was doing a study on the stolen children in that province, and she gave me a lot of concrete information, since she had access to the archives of the Provincial Council of Gerona, of the maternity and of the orphanage. Through it, I was able to find out that my biological mother was named Susan, that she was English, and apparently, there was a document signed by her, in which she renounced me (gave the baby up for adoption). There were doubts however about her signature, and the circumstances of the renouncement, but had my mother then voluntarily given me up? Was I an unwanted baby? I felt pain growing in my chest again.

In parallel, and, also, thanks to social networks and the information of the associations, I learned about the DNA analysis done by the American company *23andMe*, located in California. But thankfully, through the internet and postal service, they can and do business and testing throughout the world. Apparently, it has been very useful for many people to find out who their ancestors and relatives are and more about their origins. So, I did the test, and I waited for the results with anxiety. When my test results arrived, I discovered I had almost 1,000 relatives all over the world, cousins from the second grade to the fifth ... most of them very distant and with whom I shared a very low degree of kinship ... but something was better than nothing.

One of these relatives was Chantal M. (This name has been altered to protect a civilian who was not a client of Mr. Vila) my second cousin, who is also a doctor in genealogy and had worked a lot on our common family tree. Through her, and with her invaluable help, she was sending me more and more concrete data of our common family. She was 'stretching the genealogical thread,' as she called it, until she found my mother's sister. I became very nervous and even more anxious, because I was getting close to what I had always wanted to discover. Through social networks, I located that sister, and through her, I discovered that she also had two brothers! All of them in the United Kingdom. With more details provided by social networks and with the help of Chantal, I was able to locate the specific whereabouts of my mother.

At that time, I decided that I needed the help of a professional. I could not meet my mother, after 51 years since my birth, "*a las bravas*" (on my own, without help)."

At this point, based on information shared to us by Enrique, Julia then contacted Enrique Vila's office. She explained to him that she had heard how he specialized in performing research and professional encounter (reunion) mediations so that each party would be treated fairly and any undue stress, anxiety or even shock on anyone involved would be hopefully, avoided.

In what would be analogous to affidavits in the US, Julia stated how Enrique advised her how best to handle the encounter, so that her biological mother, whom she had never met nor knew any details about, other than those basics which she had shared in her client-mediator relationship, would not reject the reunion or resent this possible intrusion into her life as an adult. That could stir up old memories of shame, exploitation, even deceit.

Continuing now in Julia's own words from the file and her journal notes.

"Enrique Vila wrote a more formal letter, explaining the reasons and consequences of my search and meeting, reassuring my mother and letting her know how he could relate, as he, himself, was adopted. In his letter, which accompanied one of mine, in which in a much more sentimental way, I expressed what I thought, why I wanted to find her, and that I was dying to embrace her ... the wait since we sent her the letters was terrible.

I knew that Enrique had advised me not to go ahead by myself, but still, it seemed like forever. The mediation would be led by Chantal M., my distant relative, and Mr. Vila, and it couldn't happen soon enough for me.

One desperate day, I posted through Facebook to one of my sisters-in-law. I used the computer translator, because my English is very basic, but I managed to get my main points across. To my surprise, my sister-in-law answered me immediately, she reacted wonderfully and told me that she believed everything because I (she had seen my photos on Facebook), was exactly like her mother-in-law. That is, to say, my biological mother! My whole body trembled ... my sister-in-law sent me a picture of my mother finally, and I could not stop crying ... indeed, the resemblance was amazing.

From there everything accelerated. My sister-in-law spoke with her husband, my brother, and they gave her the news that I had "appeared" to Susan, my biological mother.

The first contact with her was through *WhatsApp*. I will never forget the day when I read for the first time the written words that my mother addressed to me ... that they clarified so many things about my biological mother and about me ...

[Thanks to the generosity of Julia G., and with approval by Enrique Vila, below is the first text sent by Susan to Julia, the very first words Julia read from her biological mother].

Well, I was only 19 when I met your father (EK), but I was out of that relationship soon because you were born without him knowing that I was pregnant. I must have been in denial. Fortunately, my parents were on vacation when I was also on vacation with a female friend but in a different area. I was in Lloret de Mar ... I was only there 48 hours when I went to the clinic with you. They hurried me to the convent's hospital, I was petrified. You had a quick and easy birth, but the representative asked me if there was someone I could contact and fortunately, I said my parents are also in Spain. But I think Stephanie told you those details. Then I was taken away to a different location by my parents to end our vacation. I returned to work the following Monday. I never spoke to your father again.

They took a picture of you, which was showed to your father as proof of your birth. I broke up with your father because I discovered he was married and had children. Maybe, if I had you in England and he had not been married...maybe, this would have been a very different story. I married Mick (Susan's husband) in 1971 and we've been happily married for 46 years last September. I am also pleased that they kept your name (Julie), as it means soft hair and beautiful or vivacious. From the pictures sent to me, you really are quite beautiful.

[Below is the first message from Susan's younger sister, Stephanie, Julia's biological aunt, to Julia]

Hello Julia. I'm your aunt Stephanie. Your mother's younger sister. I saw you when you were born, so beautiful. I am very happy that you are in contact with mom, we have talked about you several times over the years. You have always been in our hearts. I was delighted here with all your news. Blessed you precious one. Xx Aunt Stephanie.

In following-up on this case and the portion of the case where Enrique Vila was able to play an important mediation role towards its end in helping what eventually was an in-person reunion, some questions remained.

Was this merely a case of an unwanted pregnancy? A case of a mother who was ashamed of an adulterous affair on the part of the biological father and consequently, provided informed consent for a quick and speedy adoption?

Or was there more to the story? As Susan wrote to Julia in Spain, perhaps, she wondered, if it had happened in England in the 1960s and not the Spain of Franco, things would have been different.

We discussed these questions with Enrique and based on his insight as well as follow-up investigations we conducted on our own, we can share the following:

First, from Enrique:

"It is easy to see how Susan, Julia's biological mother, was a victim of the repressive morality of those years. An unwanted pregnancy, with an older man, who was also married. If Susan had received help and understanding, she might have been able to keep the baby Julia. But in Spain of 1967, there were very powerful forces, the church, the government, and those who profited from illegal or falsified adoptions, all of which often coerced, pressured, even threatened young, single mothers like Susan to either give up their baby voluntarily or were deceived into giving the baby to adoption. In this instance, the adoptive parents, it would seem, mostly the father, did not want their adopted daughter to ever find out about the truth and clearly, adopted the baby with false papers in an accelerated and improper if not, outright, illegal method.

We may never know how much money was paid or to whom or what role the powerful baby mafia network in Spain played in this case. But again, the Spain of 1967, was a country where it was very easy to leave a child to be adopted, almost rewarded those involved in making this decision, because immediately the baby entered into the networks of illegal, accelerated baby sales which prevailed in our country.

That's why Julia's adoptive parents never wanted to tell her the truth of her birth. That's why her father even invented the absurd false story that she was his biological daughter from his relationship with an unnamed, non-existent Belgian woman."

135

Secondly, here is a recent update from our research that everyone may find interesting:

Julia and Susan did eventually meet in-person in England very recently. In fact, Julia was excited to be able to share a picture of herself and her biological mother together on social media in October of 2019. And, as is evident, their physical resemblance is indeed, astonishing. Not so coincidentally, they both are beaming.

As Enrique noted, they continue to express thanks to him and everyone who helped them reunite and their affection is sent "across the pond" to Spain.

Chapter 6
María and Ana, from Oviedo to LA
Ted, from Madrid to Oklahoma

The following are two more cases from the files of Enrique Vila. In both instances, Mr. Vila played the role of an intermediary who helped the clients complete their search for their biological parent and to aid in facilitating what would eventually become a physical reunion. The case immediately below involves a mother and daughter, the following case is an adult son whose search for his biological mother leads him to some unexpected news.

While neither case involves any clear cut act of theft or stealing of babies, it helps illustrate how fraud and deception at the point of delivery by the hospital, nuns, nurses and doctors involved in the process makes it nearly as difficult as if the baby were actually stolen. Both cases also continue to highlight Enrique Vila's specialization in his work with victims which is helping foster a mediated and harmonious reunion when such a possibility exists.

The Case of María and Ana: A Secret Journey from Oviedo, Spain to Los Angeles, California

María VG (surname abbreviated for confidentiality of client) was a Spanish female, who lived in a small town in the province of Oviedo, in Spain. What we now know is that she was born in 1946 just after World War II ended. She grew up and became a young adult in Spain of the 1960s which was still under the repressive, dictatorial regime of Franco. Aligned with the Catholic Church they fostered and imposed upon Spanish society a rigid morality. As we have seen in prior cases in this book, in practice this frequently meant that there was a great deal of coercion and pressure imposed on young, single mothers to give up their babies as a means of "purging" their shame for having committed the sin of getting pregnant outside of the bonds of Holy Matrimony. And more often than not, when pressure, coercion and outright threats did not achieve the desired goal, then, as we have seen in so many cases, babies were simply stolen and the mother deceived into thinking her baby had died during or shortly after birth.

Of course, such morally rigid and unforgiving standards were not equally applied. Men, even those that were married, if they had an adulterous affair were not shamed or "marked" as disreputable and a sinner like their female partner. This was so, even if the other woman was much younger or even a minor. The woman who "allowed" herself to get pregnant was "marked" (1) for life and told she had only one option, to put the baby, a product of her own sinful lust, up for adoption. If she refused, she would pay a steep price, one way or the other.

When María was just 17, she found herself in just such a delicate and socially unacceptable position. She began dating a man whom she would later discover was married. In 1965, when she was just turning 20, she found out she was pregnant. She was soon ostracized by her family, and her partner, Pedro, left her upon hearing the pregnancy news. Abandoned by nearly everyone she knew, she turned to a friend, Magdalena, who accompanied her to a *Patronato de Protección*, which, as we discussed in Chapter 1, often disguised its true intentions in the rhetoric of selfless service and protection of young, single women who had nowhere else to turn, just like María. The reality was often much darker and self-serving than anyone at the time imagined. (2)

At this *Patronato*, María recalls making it clear she wanted to keep her baby no matter what. Yet, soon things were literally and figuratively out of her own hands. Documents were falsified, the name of the biological mother (María) was recorded as "unknown" and the actual birth of her daughter, Ana, was

138

inscribed as an "anonymous birth." The baby and birth were recorded in the official civil registry as having "unknown parents." In short, the network and its process of pressure, coercion, even threats were in high gear. Though, María, unlike in other cases, was not told her baby had died, she recalls feeling so much pressure and having no voice, while those in power, the nuns of the Daughters of Charity at the *Patronato*, the doctor, the nurse, went about quickly and efficiently to rid María and society of this "shameful" baby. Soon, the baby was adopted by a couple in Zaragoza, Spain who made a large "donation" to the Daughters of Charity and María returned home to her parents to live with what she had done.

María also recalls wanting to file a police report and a complaint that she was deceived and coerced, and not told her full rights as a mother. But many whom she knew, including the nuns told her that she was young, to forget it and to have more children.

Dejected, and at the time, suicidal, María recalls feeling so much shame and being "marked" in Spanish society, that she couldn't bear it. Within three years after the birth of her baby she left Spain to start a new life in Venezuela. Within time, she did meet another person with whom she married, and they had a son together. Years passed and her son became an adult, her husband passed on and she and her son eventually moved to California. María became a nationalized citizen of the United States.

In 2012, shortly after the class action lawsuit was filed on behalf of over 260 stolen babies and the Spanish media began devoting airtime to some of the more high-profile cases, her baby daughter, Ana, now also an adult, began looking for her biological mother, María. She contacted Enrique Vila to assist her in her search. Though, she had been able to accomplish much on her own, Enrique, along with a private detective who often worked cases with him, Octavio Morellá, were able to help Ana put the final pieces together. Confirming that she was indeed born in the *Patronato* run by the Daughters of Charity in Oviedo in May of 1966, they tracked down the name of her biological mother. The latter took extensive research as the name and identity was "buried" under "anonymous" in the civil registry records of the provincial government of the Asturias. By matching dates and years and births and through the process of elimination, her biological mother's full name was discovered. Next came an equally hard part, locating where she was living now, if indeed, she was still alive. In 2012, María was 66, so, Enrique and Ana were cautiously optimistic she was alive and well and only needed to be found.

What occurred next, in the words of Enrique Vila:

"Well, based on the records, we knew she (María) was originally from a small village in Asturias near Gijón. However, there was no sign of her in Spain. We followed a few leads, but they soon proved false. Where was my client's mother? We located some of her brothers, older than her, and none of them wanted to give us information about her sister, even less so to a stranger (me) who said he was looking for her because she had a long-lost daughter!

We spent a lot of time with her family, but they did not tell us anything. They did not even say they knew the story of her pregnancy and the adoption. Obviously, although the brothers were somewhat older than María, they were too young when the events occurred to know anything, and the adults had either kept absolute silence or made the siblings promise not to divulge the truth.

We stayed at it and eventually were able to find out that María was alive and lived out west in the USA, maybe California. Nothing else. We searched there and several people appeared with the surnames "VG." They were Spanish surnames, which was promising but in California there is a large Hispanic community, so the names were not as uncommon as one might imagine. After more research, we did find a handful of females but upon digging a bit more, none of these with the "VG" surname was a Spanish woman of about 66 years old. We got to talk to some citizens of San Francisco and San Diego who had her same last name in the hopes of finding a relative, but that didn't pan out either.

We only knew that María VG was in California, that was confirmed by all her Spanish relatives, and that she almost never visited Spain. Either she couldn't afford to travel or perhaps, had no desire to return to her place of birth. I began to suspect that there may be a painful history that was being kept hidden for years. And, maybe the real reason behind her move to the USA.

After several attempts and negotiations, and a well-intentioned "fib" to one of her sisters, we got a current address for María. Apparently, she was living in North Hollywood, Los Angeles.

A few days later, as soon as my agenda allowed, I traveled to the USA to conduct the search and mediation. This part of the process is always exciting and a bit nerve-racking. To tell a stranger, that her daughter is waiting for her, that she wants to meet her in person, can be devastating even traumatic for the mother, depending on the circumstances of why the baby was put up for adoption or even stolen. Either way, it is a delicate situation with risk. In addition, such important news must always be given in person, that is my policy.

After an exhausting 13-hour trip to Los Angeles, I finally found myself in LA, drained but still excited to play my part in this possible reunion. I headed to the address we had been given. It was the only clue. North Hollywood is a neighborhood comprised mostly of simple residential blocks of two floors, rectangular roads, full of art galleries and sound studios. It is also a neighborhood with a considerable population of residents of Hispanic origin, many from Mexico. (3)

I spent nearly two whole days inside the Toyota car I had rented, watching María's house. It seemed obviously closed. I called her relatives from Spain again and I passed myself off as a writer (there I did not lie), a friend of the family's grandfather (whose identity I had previously known in my research), who wanted to deliver a gift in person to María, and who happened to be in Los Angeles for other events. I must be convincing as one of the sisters gave me María's cell phone number. I soon called, and finally I heard the voice of my client's mother. I maintained my cover story and we set a day and time when I could deliver the gift in person. I did not have much time, because I could not stay in the US for many days, and I needed to meet her soon and give her the bombshell news."

Here, as Enrique made clear to us, things almost became untracked forever.

"She told me to leave the gift in Los Angeles, that she would pick it up, because at that time she was with her son in San Jose, a town near San Francisco, almost 380 miles from Los Angeles. It could not be. I was so close, yet so far. She wasn't even in Los Angeles. I was able to finally get her to at least give me her son's address so I could mail the gift there as she was visiting her son and could not receive anyone and she did not want to make me make such a long trip.

Of course, I could not stop now, not when I was this close on behalf of Ana. I crossed the Californian desert with my rental Toyota and arrived in San Jose exhausted. I looked for the address María had given me and waited patiently in the car. Later, I knocked on the door keeping my role as a writer family friend but there was no answer. The plane was leaving the next day from LAX, and I did not want delays, because in Spain there were also some very urgent matters waiting for me. Where could María be? I was waiting for her for more than half a day, I asked some neighbors, and nobody knew anything. Maybe, she was on a trip for several days with her American son. I started to have doubts whether this was ever going to take place.

When it was getting dark, I was almost going to give up. I knocked one last time and I heard a noise in the house, but no one opened. Perhaps, I thought, the woman had suspected my true intentions, and would never receive me. When I was back in my car which was parked on the sidewalk in front of the son's house, the door finally opened and María appeared. She was a jovial-looking woman with blond hair, glasses, and a friendly face. I approached her, I greeted her, and she seemed delighted to receive a visitor from Spain.

'Dear lady, I've lied a bit, I'm a writer, I'm going to give you some books (I handed her a couple of my works), but I'm here for something else, on behalf of someone from Spain who wants to come but only after we are able to talk.'

The woman's face changed. Forty-six long years in silence. I looked at her eyes and saw a very special glow. She leaned on me, pushed me further away from the door, and asked me for discretion. I was excited, of course she knew why I was there. So long waiting and there I was, with the news that her daughter was looking for her. The questions and emotions were crowded, I was enthusiastic myself and I understood those feelings, as I was also looking for my biological mother.

I told María everything I could, but I left almost the whole story to be told by Ana, her daughter. I handed her a handwritten letter, which I brought from Spain, and she became very emotional. It was a preview of what would come next. María was very kind, and apologized, and was somewhat embarrassed for not inviting me inside. But, as she quickly explained, 'He does not know anything about my daughter, his Spanish sister.' I respected her wishes but left pleased, feeling confident that a real reunion between mother and daughter after so many years, was fully in motion.

And that motion, that progress did lead to an in-person reunion. In fact, they have been able to visit each other several times, though time, distance and cost (traveling from Zaragoza, Spain to Los Angeles, California) limits their visits. However, they have updated me and informed me that they talk often, they write, they videoconference each other and both still feel there remains much to talk about, discuss and share, as only mothers and daughters are able to, after all.

Both seem happy. María found the daughter she never really wanted to give up but felt she was given no choice. Ana found her true origins. I hope they have enough time to recover what was lost. They now have more than so many less fortunate."

The Mysterious Case of Ted M., of Oklahoma, USA by way of Madrid, Spain.

While this case is still not fully resolved, below is what we now know, in part from Enrique's case notes, his own recollection, and our joint research. The following is Enrique's narration of Ted's story unless otherwise noted:

"**Ted** was born in 1962 at the Santa Cristina Hospital in Madrid, to a Spanish mother. Almost immediately after the birth, he was adopted to an American couple who lived in Spain and worked at a US military base in Madrid. As a result of a formal agreement between Spain and the USA in the aftermath of World War II (Madrid Pact of 1953), there was a significant presence of Americans in Madrid as well as other areas of Spain on a permanent basis. (4)

Many American families created strong ties with Spain and the Spanish people as a result of such close proximity and this

144

alliance of friendship between the two nations. In the case of Ted's parents, it could be said that they benefitted not only from this Pact but when it came to adopting a baby, they certainly benefitted from the illegal network of baby selling which was prevalent in Spain at that time. The adoptive parents of Ted found that they could not have children naturally. They asked around and soon got connected with the network, the baby mafia, in Spain. They discovered it would not cost that much, was obviously much quicker to get it done than through any normal, legal process and no questions would be asked. From what we know, though, these Americans were hesitant. They wanted to do things proper and legal. They did not want to "buy" a baby. However, they were anxious to be parents. They asked at the American Embassy in Madrid, and there they were connected to a lawyer who helped in the consular work in the Spanish State. This lawyer redirected them in turn to another lawyer well known in the capital, who was responsible for the issue of adoptions, and had a hand in many of the maternity hospitals in Madrid and the adoptions from these hospitals.

Based on records, notes and testimonials recovered, Ted's future adoptive parents met with an adoption "broker" in Madrid and told him they wanted to, as much as possible, have the adoption be handled legally. He assured them that, at that time in Spain, the adoption was something of an *a la carte* process, and it was all lawful. He also informed them that it was expected, even required, that they make a significant "donation" to an institution like the Daughters of Charity. He assured them that if such a donation was made then the process (to adopt) would be accelerated. Ultimately, it appears that a donation was, in fact, made to the Daughters of Charity in Madrid and, they were told, it would go to the biological mother who was single and of humble means. The Americans entered the game, because they wanted to be parents and this lawyer, who they trusted, assured them that everything was going to be legal.

So, it is at least conceivable that in this case, the adoptive parents were truly unaware they were soon "knee-deep" in the ongoing mafia, the baby stealing and buying network in Spain. Many years later, in retrospect, so much about this network and how it operated has been uncovered, but at that time (1960s) especially to non-Spaniards unfamiliar with Spain's true system of adoption, it most likely seemed if not typical then certainly "normal" for Spain.

Sadly though, normal for Spain at this time was a highly corrupt, self-serving and deceitful system at work. In this case, Sister María Gómez Valbuena, who would later be the first nun to be indicted on baby stealing criminal charges spanning several decades, was one of the primary operatives. She was the titular head of the Santa Cristina hospital where Ted was born and by all accounts, coordinated the illegal adoption of Ted to his adoptive parents who then left their work at the American military base and returned to the United States to raise their baby in the State of Oklahoma. Also, regrettably, before Gómez Valbuena was forced to answer for her many alleged crimes in a court of law, she died just days after her initial indictment. There continues to be a growing contingent of Spaniards who refuse to believe she actually died, citing her immediate cremation, seen as a sin in the Catholic Church, as evidence her death was merely a hoax, a cover, to spirit her out of Spain and away from the inquiring spotlight.

Regardless of the circumstances surrounding her death, when she was alive, she was, as many of her co-workers, staff and fellow nuns have attested to, a commanding, authoritative figure."

Supplementing Enrique's notes and recollections are the following, translated from Spanish articles and sources:

Regarding Sor María, Montse S., an assistant at the Santa Cristina Hospital, recalls her as, "seemingly knowing everyone, always in contact with anyone and everyone involved in adopting babies." Fellow nuns who have asked still to remain anonymous have also added that Sister María would constantly review the hospital admittance forms, searching for younger, single and pregnant mothers. She targeted them, knowing they were the most vulnerable, shared a nun who claims to have worked with Gómez Valbuena for over two decades.

Mila G., a trained midwife who studied and worked for a time at the Santa Cristina Hospital remembers that Sister María was "obsessed with finding single, pregnant women," often remarking to staff to "be on the lookout for young, single mothers," asking us, "What are these women going to do with these babies anyways? They know nothing. It is best if they give their babies up for adoption."

According to Mila, after identifying the young mothers who seemed most vulnerable and had the greatest potential to give up their babies, she (Sister María) would begin to apply pressure and raise doubt in the minds of these already frightened and vulnerable girls, she would do this daily, without stopping until they broke. She would ask probing questions like "Have you thought that this child could have a future if you would allow him to leave with a good family, but what future could this child have with you, a single, poor mother with no future?" She would play on their fears with statements like, "You see that no one is here for you, you are alone, how can you possible care for your baby, don't be selfish and foolish, give him up so he has a chance in life."

"Like a spider, she was spinning her web," explains Mila. "These mothers were brainwashed so by the time the delivery came, these doubts were already planted, along with heavy drugs which made reasoning and thinking clearly difficult, so that in the

147

end, many agreed and signed the consent to give their children." She and other co-workers have since shared that while many soon regretted their decision and asked, even begged to see and have their baby before the adoption was formalized, Gómez Valbuena would simply inform them that the papers had been signed and they were too late and to stop crying and whining like little, silly schoolgirls.

Ignacia M. still has painful memories of what she saw when she worked at Santa Cristina under the direction of the Nun Gómez Valbuena. "I have seen many women cry. And kick, and scream and even punch their beds, begging to see their newborn babies. Nuns and nurses would tell these mothers that their baby had died." Ignacia continues, "Sister María had trained her staff well and they refused to tell these mothers what had really happened, that their babies had been taken away to those with money who bought these babies on demand." (5)

In addition to case files like Enrique's, articles like those cited above, as well as our own research, we can also share that across Spain many of these "adoptions on demand" were not inexpensive. Adopting parents were charged between 50,000 to 1,000,000 pesetas (between about $350 USD to nearly $7,000 USD). Controlling for inflation, this would calculate to about $2,800 to $22,000 today. This was not a game open to just anyone. Valbuena told couples seeking babies that these donations (costs charged) were to cover the costs of having to care for the mother. Yet, these hospitals were subsidized by the government and/or supported by the church along with governmental funding. Testimonials now public also make clear from both workers and mothers across Spain that the absolute bare minimum was spent on the care of these young mothers and they were discharged almost immediately upon delivery of their baby even if they still needed care or to properly recover.

148

Mari S., who also worked under the Nun Gómez Valbuena, recalls a time where she saw into the office of Valbuena who by accident, had this one time left her door slightly ajar as she met with a couple who sought a baby. "There was a stack of money on the desk, about $250,000 pesetas and Sister María was telling them that 'one' was almost ready and that for a bit more perhaps she could even speed up the transfer of the baby." (6)

This then was the baby buying network across Spain at the time when Ted's adoptive parents sought to adopt a baby and even more specifically, this was the ongoing baby buying operation at Santa Cristina under the direction of the Nun Gómez Valbuena.

As Enrique notes, for reasons which will soon become apparent, he cannot say for sure if Ted's parents knew what was or was not legal in Spain at the time nor the true intention of Ted's biological mother, whether she of her own free will with a clear mind gave her baby up for adoption, we can conclude with no uncertainty, that money was exchanged between Ted's adoptive parents and Sister María. As public records, affidavits and testimonies collected in preparation for the trial of the Nun Gómez Valbuena (which never happened due to her death), make clear, to imagine any such adoption could occur at Santa Cristina without such a direct payment being made to her is to simply engage in unfounded fantasy. In short, she headed up the operation. (7)

[Enrique's narration continues] "As for the Ted M., well, he grew up like most children in the United States. He went to school, played with friends, enjoyed sports and as soon as he was old enough to understand it, he was told of his adopted status. His parents did not make any effort to hide this reality from him. Like many adopted children, once they are told or discover this status, especially as adults, they become curious and often want to find out more about their biological parents and any blood related relatives. Ted was no different. He also wanted to know more of

149

his original ancestry. While he was raised as an American, he also knew he was adopted as a baby in Spain and he wanted to know more about his background.

Now an adult, he contacted a graduate student he knew of who was doing a thesis on illegal adoptions in Spain, Marta T., and, she in turn, recommended that Ted contact me in the hopes I could perhaps help locate his mother and aid in facilitating a reunion. Ted M. wrote me an email requesting my help and telling me what he knew or had been able to confirm through his own search. He sent me the documentation of his birth, and I discovered that, in it, the name of his biological mother, a woman from Málaga who had given birth to him in 1962 in Madrid was falsified, and as has been explained previously, this was quite common in many such cases.

We were able to verify that the Spanish surnames were real and common in the area of Andalusia. We reached out to our network of contacts and were able to expand the scope of the search to include possible relatives. We soon discovered several of Ted's nephews alive. We were optimistic that we would soon be able to locate Ted's biological mother.

But sadly, based on information we were able to get from documents of related family members we confirmed that his biological mother, Josefa C. R., who was born in 1925 had died just a few years before we began our search. However, we were able to identify a surviving family member. Josefa had a daughter, María José, who was born just a few years before Ted. In the case of María José, Josefa, her mother, had registered this baby with her own last name exclusively, no name of the biological father was provided or registered on the birth certificate. The nephews which we were able to locate were the children of Ted's biological sister, María José.

150

The first actual words I got from a family member of Ted's was Lourdes, Ted's niece (daughter of María José, Ted's sister), and she confirmed all my information. She also told me that she had shown a picture of Ted to her own mother (María José) and she told her very excitedly, that my client (Ted) reminded her of the traits of the biological mother (Josefa) who had died a few years before.

A few weeks after finding his family, Ted traveled with his wife from the USA to Madrid and was able to embrace his biological living relatives. After the torrent of emotions, we all began to speculate about the truth of his birth. No one really knows what happened, because although they knew of Ted's birth, the real circumstances of it were taken by his mother to her grave.

But based on the information from Ted, the research we did and what Ted's nieces and nephews were able to confirm for us, this much we know:

That his biological mother, Josefa, worked in Madrid and was a young, single mother with a 4-year-old daughter at the time of Ted's birth. She was already a "marked" woman in the ultra-conservative and catholic Spanish society. She also, as we have examined, gave birth at the Santa Cristina hospital run by Sister María Gómez Valbuena, one of the most allegedly corrupt and notorious baby-stealing and selling figure throughout Spain. The allegations of her crimes and the span of time which they allegedly took place rival even that of Dr. Vela

It is just as conceivable to conclude that Josefa, who already had shown courage and devotion to her first child as a single, young mother, was coerced or deceived into giving up Ted as a baby as it is to conclude, as we have, that Ted's adoptive parents paid for a speedy and improper adoption of Ted, knowingly or not.

Why would Josefa have voluntarily given up Ted as a baby, her first-born son and chosen to never see him again?"

We will never know.

Even more lamentably, neither will her son.

In the next chapter (Chapter 7) we dig even deeper into this baby stealing issue with the help of several renowned experts.

Chapter 7
The Experts Speak Out

In conducting the many interviews with stolen baby victims, we did, dating back to 2015, and then all the on-camera interviews we conducted during 2018 and 2019, several things jumped out at us. It was impossible not to notice the similarity of the stories shared by so many of the victims regardless of who we interviewed or where we filmed. We would get chills when we would hear victims tell us how doctors, nurses or nuns would tell them "Forget about your baby. You are young. You can have more. Stop crying."

As we've noted before, it was as if there was some type of criminal handbook or manual which was shared by all those involved in these crimes and each memorized their lines and never strayed from the pre-approved script. This mafia, as Enrique and so many others we spoke to called it, was eerily similar in how it conducted these thefts no matter where they occurred.

While those we spoke with were incredibly open and engaging despite their loss and suffering, we had completely opposite experiences when we tried to talk with those who were in positions of responsibility and authority in Spain and who were, at least on paper, supposed to be seeking the truth. For example, despite our contacting prosecutors across Spain no one would talk to us, on or off camera. In one instance, through a personal, family contact in Spain, we were able to get some written questions to a prosecutor (*Fiscal*) which dealt with the process of why and when cases brought to them about stolen babies are closed. But even in this instance, we hit a wall of silence. Check our website, we were told. We did. It had nothing of any relevance to any of our questions. We followed up and asked again, by phone, email and in-person. Drop the matter, we were told or face consequences.

One time we were standing on a public street in Madrid filming an exterior shot of a famous church run clinic where several alleged cases of stolen babies had occurred. It was midday and for all they knew we could have been typical tourists. A woman came from inside the clinic though and accosted us on the street. How dare we film them, she angrily asked us. We had no right to do this and unless we left, she would call the police. We told her we were doing nothing illegal, merely standing on a public street filming the outside of a building. She cursed us. We stayed put and we never did see any police come. But the lesson was clear, at least to us, the guilty always have more to hide than the innocent. (1)

Another time, we were in a cemetery in Alicante on a Sunday. We were filming some exterior shots and then some close-up shots of markers and statues which honored the fallen soldiers of the Spanish Civil War. Again, we were accosted. This time by a worker who got out of his truck and yelled at us to put away our cameras and that it was forbidden. We were breaking a national law he said by taking pictures or filming in a cemetery. We had never heard of such a law. What if we wanted to take pictures of a family stone or grave, then what, was he going to have us arrested for that? Again, we were threatened with police action. We stayed, he left, and no police arrived to arrest us for the alleged crime of taking pictures or filming in a public cemetery. (2)

Of course, there is no such law, at least not to our knowledge. But it again drove home the continued state of near paranoia which so many still have in Spain when it comes to the past and to having anyone chronicle this past.

In the *Valle de los Caídos*, an awe-inspiring and incredible monument built literally by the forced labor of former Republican

154

soldiers to honor Franco and the church, we saw how every day fresh flowers are placed at the tombstone of the dictator Franco inside this massive public exhibit. We also saw a guard admonish schoolchildren for standing either too close or directly on the tombstone of Franco. The guard told us how there is no respect for great leaders anymore in Spain and pointed to the rain which drips down from cracks in the ceiling and that the Government no longer provides the money to properly fix or even maintain this monument. It is, she told us, a true tragedy and a sign of how far Spain has fallen over the years and the disrespect for leadership that is now prevalent. (3)

To gain further insight into this continued mentality of secrecy and even paranoia over its past and to discuss what needs to happen next for victims to achieve justice, we spoke with **Carmen del Mazo**, a former nun of the Daughters of Charity who worked at the notorious Santa Cristina (O'Donnell) hospital in Madrid, **María José Esteso**, an investigative journalist and author, **Francisco González de Tena**, a famed sociologist and author and **Pablo Rosser**, a historian who works in the historical memory and cultural heritage section for the city of Alicante.

We met with Carmen del Mazo, appropriately enough, in front of a church in Madrid. Carmen is a former nun, who worked for years with the Daughters of Charity. She also worked at the Santa Cristina hospital during the time when Sister María Gómez Valbuena was the Mother Superior or head of the nuns at that institution. This hospital, also known as "O'Donnell," for the street on which it is located in Madrid, is notorious for the alleged crimes of baby stealing and selling which took place for decades. You will recall that this is the same hospital where Ted G., (his case appears in Chapter 6) was born and then sold to his adoptive parents in 1966.

155

We weren't sure how this meeting was going to go. Would Carmen be protective of the church? After all, she had devoted her life to its work and had answered its calling at a young age. Or, would the fact that she is a former nun mean she was no longer a believer or just that she could not go on condoning things she had been made to do as a nun? Something else?

We soon got our answer.

"I had friends, fellow nuns, who worked at O'Donnell full time. I would go there on my days off from other service I was doing for the Daughters of Charity, most of the time it was on a Sunday. I would help care for the newborn babies and the mothers who were about to deliver or who had just delivered and were recovering. We were instructed though, and this came from the top (Sister María), that we were forbidden from going on a certain floor of the hospital. We all knew this was where the babies were taken away from the mothers. Other nuns would talk and say how single mothers should not be allowed to keep their babies. That the church was clear on this point. A baby must be raised within a family that had a father and mother and be bound by marriage, I would think, 'But what about a widow? She would raise her children without their father. Why then, would a single mother be forbidden from doing the same thing?'

Even if a single mother had placed her baby in our care while she tried to find work or had a job and could not visit every day, I would hear other nuns say how they hoped the mother would not come back for a while so that the child could be registered as abandoned and given up for adoption. This, many believed was what the Mother Superior preferred, to always have enough babies to fill the demand.

One time I was told to prepare a baby for adoption and then told to bring the child to the adoptive parents, which I did. At the time I guess I thought it was all legal, but still I wondered. Because not long after, the mother, who we were told was a beggar or a prostitute and that the father was in jail, came to O'Donnell and asked for her baby. She was told she could not see the baby because it had a high fever and was isolated for fear it could spread to other babies. There were similar instances and each time similar excuses were given to the mother wanting to see her baby. This way when enough time had elapsed, they could then show that the mother and baby had not been together for several weeks or a few months and then could register the baby as abandoned and sell it to adoptive parents.

Our superiors knew what they were doing. Many of us (nuns) I think had doubts and didn't want to believe but after a while it became too clear. I have seen too much documentation falsified and have heard too many sad stories that were too much like what I had witnessed not to be true. It saddens me that the church does not recognize the terrible role it played in this dark chapter of the church and of Spain. They should ask for forgiveness and open its records to help so many victims find the truth and find peace before it is too late.

I am very hurt that the church does not at least recognize the hurt it has caused to so many.

It is why I had to leave and turn away from my devotion. I could no longer live with what it had done."

Since leaving the Daughters of Charity and deciding to no longer be a nun, Carmen has actively worked on behalf of a number of stolen baby victims in their search. She recently was one of several to meet with *Monseñor* Blázquez, the President of the Spanish Episcopal Conference (a powerful group representing many churches and parishioners or followers).

"He promised that he would "open doors" for people. But he was vague. We wanted to know the specifics. He finally said that he would allow the Bishops to make these decisions and work on the regional and local level. But once they find out it is for stolen baby victims then many certificates and records are being denied.

The *Monseñor* has told us that it is the Judiciary that must investigate and help us but they (Judiciary) tell us their hands are tied without the church opening its records. They protect each other.

I have tried to speak with the Mother Superior at O'Donnell to provide records for victims. She only says that it happened a long time ago and it is not her fault. We are not trying to blame those like her in charge now, but we believe this dark side of the church's past must be confronted and it must ask for forgiveness. But the victims, the mothers, they deserve more. Many have suffered, many have had to go to psychiatrists just to function in daily life, they are re-victimized by church denials and delays.

It is similar to the pedophilia cases in the Catholic Church and predatory priests. Denying the truth, covering it up, lying about it or just moving the pedophile priest from church to church solves nothing. It only violates victims again and again. We want the church to ask for forgiveness, recognize what it has done but we need more, they need to open all records so that cases cannot be closed (*archivado*) based on no evidence.

But it is not just the church. Judges and prosecutors in Spain do nothing. I have no doubt that many judges have illegally adopted, bought babies even while they closed the cases of victims who come to them for justice. In Spain, judges and prosecutors have a great deal of power and do not want to be exposed themselves for being part of the problem."

Carmen paused here as we asked her where she sees this problem going, does she see hope? In the summer of 2018 Spain had ousted its conservative leader, Mariano Rajoy and had installed a more liberal leader, Pedro Sánchez. (4)

"Well, maybe the political air is changing, and the government will support victims more now. But without church cooperation, justice will always be limited. We have written the Pope, asking him to admonish the Spanish Church and order them to fully cooperate. But he has not answered our pleas.

And the Daughters of Charity, who were in every hospital and clinic and who worked with so many congregations, has so much it can do and open for victims, records, documents, notebooks, allow others to give testimony, but they stay silent. They say much has been destroyed in fires, floods, other disasters.

We wrote here in Spain to the Nuncio *Monseñor* Rouco Varela to take steps to help. He only responded by calling on us to pray for the Pope. He ignored everything in our letter.

The law has been changed here in Spain and it has ordered the church to open its files and provide records to victims. But the church refuses. They hope that victims either die or simply give up their search. And the government refuses to enforce its law.

I pray they do what is right before it is too late to matter."

María José Esteso, an investigative journalist who has written a number of articles for magazines and journals in Spain as well as books which chronicle how and when baby stealing began, also holds both the Catholic Church and the Spanish Government accountable for these crimes. As she says, "Where one begins, and the other ends is nearly indistinguishable. They entered into a mutually beneficial alliance, that, in many ways, continues on even today."

When we shared part of what Carmen had told us and the role of nuns in the taking of babies to María José, she was far from surprised. "I would have been surprised only if she had told you something different," she replied. She explained how when she and other journalists had begun to construct the timeframe of these baby thefts, they noted how, when the construction of new

159

hospitals began to boom in the mid-1960s in Spain and the laws made giving birth in hospitals under doctor care mandatory, there were many stories being shared from different mothers across Spain. Mothers, who, while they did not know each other, told very similar details. "In short," María José said, "Mothers shared how others would tell them not to go to these hospitals…because babies disappear from them and never return."

When we met with María José in Madrid in the late summer of 2018, the trial of Dr. Vela was nearing. She expressed some optimism at the outcome but feared that, like Sister María Gómez Valbuena before him, something would intervene to prevent true justice from happening. "Spain has many unexplained such phenomenon," she noted.

For the documentary film, María José went into a detailed description of the baby stealing network or the mafia, as Enrique Vila and others called it, which started as a means to repress and punish the so-called 'reds' or enemies of Franco in the late 1930s. Then, decades later, transformed mostly into simply a profit-making business, with babies as the commodity in demand and those in the mafia ensuring there was a constant flow of supply to meet this seemingly unlimited demand. Both in Spain and beyond, to countries like the USA.

María José noted how this baby stealing and selling for profit especially boomed between the late 1960s and into the early 1980s. This, she noted, "coincides with the time when many doctors are moving into private practice after having been trained under the Franco Regime, laws were changed to make gynecologist care mandatory, and again, both arenas are utterly dominated by male doctors from the Francoist times. They then assume positions of responsibility at universities and medical schools where doctors and gynecologists are being trained, hospitals, clinics and governmental departments which

160

supposedly oversee the medical industry. It is not hard to see how these changes and personnel are correlated with the incredible increase of supposed baby deaths during these years due to things like 'ear infections' or 'unexplained causes.' Yet, at the same time we hear of cases from mothers who are not allowed by their male doctors to see their baby or how babies are brought to incubators and fathers forbidden from viewing their newborn baby. Even stories like how gynecologists like Dr. Vela were allegedly showing mothers dead frozen babies and lying to them that it is their baby when they were selling their babies out the back door."

As we've discussed in chapter 1, María José reaffirmed that there was no doubt that these medical doctors though, did not work alone.

"They did not act alone. There are a group of actors that are always repeated. Notary Publics who knowingly sign falsified and forged documents, nurses and midwives who falsify hospital and clinic records and deceive mothers about their newborn babies, nuns of course, who play a huge role in directing this entire operation. Those like Sister Gómez Valbuena who coordinate the network to ensure the stolen baby gets to its buyer, even taxi drivers who are paid to transport stolen babies, and funeral parlor directors who know the box or coffin they are being paid to bury is empty. They all play their part in this charade, this criminal network because they all benefit from the theft of the mother's baby. They all work to make sure it is nearly impossible to ever uncover the truth.

Then, if it does go to a judge or prosecutor, many of them had illegally adopted children or knew family members who had, so they dismiss cases or close them even when evidence exists, and the victim pleads for justice. This didn't just happen under Franco, it kept happening as Spain became a democracy in the early 1980s.

What has surprised Spanish society is that it kept happening well into the 1990s and even early 2000s."

María José, like Carmen, also spoke of the need for the guilty to ask for forgiveness. But in this instance, she put her focus squarely on the Spanish Government. "The state must ask for forgiveness. For decades they have been co-conspirators in a plot to steal babies and sell them then actively cover-up the truth and now, to make it nearly impossible for victims to properly have their cases investigated and adjudicated."

We spoke with María José about other places that have seen abuses perpetrated upon their own citizens, as in the dictatorship years ago in Argentina.

María José drew a distinction between places like that and Spain.

"There (Argentina) the government admitted its role, apologized and held special tribunals to seek the truth. Victims had access to specialized police, specialized investigators and specialized courts to hear their cases. Here, in Spain, after 40 years of the Franco dictatorship and 40 years of democracy, we still have nothing like this for victims. Cases are assigned in a decentralized way, so all the discretion is in the hands of local prosecutors and judges who simply close cases at their pleasure."

While María José had some optimism that with a less conservative government heading Spain things could change, she also said that past experience forced her to be realistic.

"If in two years things don't change dramatically, I fear they never will."

Francisco González de Tena shares many of the same concerns which María José shared. A sociologist by training, Francisco has also written extensively on the Franco years and on the network and coordinated operation of baby stealing which existed in Spain for decades. Not surprisingly, he spoke with us

162

about the significance of powerful cultural and religious symbolism used by those in power to both perpetuate the crimes and to intimidate and coerce anyone who dared stand up to them. "The church in Spain was never innocent. They acted with impunity. They knew that the symbols of the church were worshipped, glorified and feared in Spain. And they used this power as a shield against the victims and anyone who tried to discover the truth.

The very concept of authority - the white coat of the doctor, the white or grey habit of the nun, the cross, the ceremonial garb of the priests and bishops were all displayed as a means to keep the citizenry at a distance. To silence them. To cow them into submission. This is why it took so long for victims to realize that they were not alone, that there were others who were told the same lies, deceived by the same process. Because nuns forbade them to talk to anyone, forbade husbands to open empty boxes filled with sand when these were supposed to be their dead babies.

Even nuns who were carrying newborn babies clearly not their own, in baskets or draped in blankets as they boarded trains or buses or even planes to travel to other countries did so with impunity. No one dared question these representatives of the church even though they were not carrying out God's will but the will of the network which worshipped greed and money."

It would be naïve of anyone, Francisco told us to believe that these cases of stolen babies were somehow isolated in nature. "For the cases to be so similar, even those where babies were illegally sold and smuggled out of Spain to places like the USA, Venezuela, Argentina, Brazil, Germany, Sweden, France, and many other places, there had to be an organization. Someone was conveying how to accomplish these crimes smoothly and without any problems."

Like Carmen, Francisco sees several major obstacles in the way of victims to ever reach justice.

"The continued reliance on *concordats* between Spain and the Vatican (agreements which allow for the church to retain and not turn over many archived adoption and family records) will help allow the church to hide in the sand unless these are overturned and they should be. The difficulty which victims face in conducting their own investigations and the unreliability of DNA laboratories here in Spain, and of course, the church in Spain must be cleaned up. Their house is filthy, and their hands are covered with the blood of the newborns which they stole from mothers."

As for any possible conviction of the accused Dr. Vela, Francisco simply added, "He (Vela) is nothing. He is not important. But a conviction would at least break the glass which covers the socialization of silence and fear in Spain. Maybe, once there are enough voices then they cannot silence all of us."

Pablo Rosser, the head of the cultural heritage section for the *Ayuntamiento* (city hall) of Alicante, a historian who works for the city of Alicante (Spain) reminded us not only of the massive destruction of so many cities throughout Spain during the civil war like Barcelona, Madrid and Alicante, one of the last Republican opposition holdouts, but also of the powerful tri-partite alliance which rose up from this war. An alliance which was so instrumental in perpetuating the network of baby stealing.

"Who participated in the plot to steal babies? There are three powers, right from the start. The political, the military and the religion. The military which punished the opposition survivors and their offspring either by executing them and leaving them in ditches or in unmarked, mass graves or by stealing their babies and giving them to those loyal to Franco. The politicians who provided political cover and laws which allowed the baby stealing, and they kept many children for themselves. And the religious

164

powers, the church, which used its own servants, the nuns to infiltrate and dominate the hospitals, the clinics, the daycares, to steal babies and deceive mothers."

Pablo shared many specific consequences of the war on Alicante and the impact on its society for decades after. In particular, he told us that "Babies were being taken out of Alicante and sold to the highest bidders like bags of oranges. Alicante babies ended up being taken to Chile, for example, because of the close relationship which the dictator Franco had with the Chilean dictator Pinochet. (5) This, was similar throughout Spain, only the final destination changed but the web, the mafia, did not change, neither in its methods nor in its greed."

One of the continuing issues which face both stolen baby victims and surviving families of those killed or executed during the Spanish Civil War is in identifying the bodies of the deceased. Pablo left us with this final thought.

"We have to remember, we (Spain) are the nation with the second highest number of citizens who have disappeared or died with no marked grave or indication. Cambodia is the only country with a higher total than Spain. We still have ditches alongside roads with unidentified skeletal remains of victims. With the passage of new laws and of the Historical Memory Act, we are making progress in this area and victims can file for and get a judicial order to have an exhumation (public or private) to confirm whether a loved one is buried where they have been told or if there is some aberration or even fraud. It is at least a step towards finally moving forward from the horror of the war and of the violation of so many mothers and their babies these past several decades."

We posed the same question to each of our experts:

What happens next, do victims have any hope of ever achieving truth, reconciliation and justice?

Francisco: "Even with new laws that have been proposed to assist victims in some small ways, it remains a very complicated and difficult issue. Because it is Spain, because it deals with God in what remains a Catholic nation, because all the guilty ones that committed these crimes over many years did so with complete liberty and impunity. They knew they had nothing to fear. The dictator and the church didn't just know what was happening, they took part, they supported it. We have found burnt archives, shredded files, intentional flooding, all done to destroy evidence. They intentionally changed the last names. Boys were inscribed as girls and vice-versa to make detection of the crime almost impossible. Even the location of the birth was changed and falsified.

So, what is the last hope? DNA testing. But with over 300,000 people still either searching or many not even knowing they were stolen, why would many even think to do a DNA test?"

Pablo: "It will be difficult because of the super-structure which continues today and which is the descendant of the dictator Franco, and there remains no appetite for many of these in power to uncover the past even if it means allowing so many to heal. This regime which supposedly ended in 1975 has never fully ended, the darker power of this regime continues, even today.

The wound will finally close only when all of the mass and unmarked graves, and the bodies are returned to their families with honors, as those who were killed in war, and when all stolen baby victims finally get access to records and archives to which they have the right to access to find loved ones. This will go a long way to helping everyone heal. But the current structure still resists, still fights this closure."

María José: "Well, (as of 2018) there are over 2,000 official complaints or cases filed in courts around Spain but the judiciary and *Fiscalía General* (Top Prosecutor) are clever, they dilute these cases by not centralizing or joining them together. This way, they can slowly dismiss or prematurely close these cases, even with evidence, on a local basis and it makes it difficult for victims to make this a national issue which it is, and to gain full media attention across Spain. By my count, only 10 of these over 2,000 cases have any chance to be fully reviewed given how our laws and courts approach such cases.

It remains an upside-down world though, we do have new hope with some new leadership which may be more empathetic to victims, but we have seen promises made and then those same promises broken before."

In the next chapter, we get to know the courageous woman at the center of the legal storm in the trial of Dr. Vela.

Chapter 8
INÉS MADRIGAL
PART I

When we were doing the bulk of the on-site filming in Spain for our documentary in the summer of 2018, the coming trial of Dr. Vela, a retired gynecologist, accused of stealing hundreds if not thousands of babies over five decades, was fast approaching. This trial was unprecedented in the history of Spain. If, convicted, this would mark the first time someone, anyone, would actually face incarceration for crimes related to the decades long stealing and selling of babies, forging and falsification of official records and intentional deception of biological parents as to the status of their babies. A few years prior, as discussed in this book, Sister María Gómez Valbuena was indicted on but never actually faced trial for similar crimes, as she died just days after her initial court arraignment.

So, as stolen baby victims awaited the coming trial with a great deal of anticipation, anxiety and cautious optimism, we sat down with Dr. Vela's accuser, Inés Madrigal. Armed with evidence and documents she claims are falsified records with Dr. Vela's signature and a powerful testimony from her adoptive mother who directly met Vela during the adoption process, Inés was the first one to take an individual stolen baby case accusation this far.

Before she faced the court inquisitors in Madrid, she generously agreed to give us an exclusive one-on-one interview for our cameras.

"It's the story of your life and you feel certain things and wonder about things even before you know for sure. When I was very young, I remember kids calling me "the adopted girl" at school. I didn't even have any idea what that meant but the way they said it, I knew it must be bad. I told my mother and she got very upset, she grabbed my hand and took a frame we had on the living room wall down and said, 'Look at this.' It was a framed copy of the Civil Registry of my birth and had all the dates, names and place involved with my birth. I also remember my mother telling the parents of these children who called me this name that if they didn't stop, she would file a police report.

What I know today is that in my small town, many of the parents knew I was adopted, that my mother, who was much older when I was brought home, had never been visibly pregnant. The parents must have told their kids who then teased me.

Growing up, there were some things I began wondering about. How I didn't look like my parents or how, when we'd be at family gatherings there would be no real affection or love like I'd see with other families. Except for one aunt who would pay attention to me all the others would make me feel invisible...or, well, like I wasn't really a part of the family.

I kept these feelings and these thoughts to myself, even until I was 18 because I was a happy person, positive, fun and wanted to enjoy life. But when I turned 18, my mother had a strong crisis, a separation with my father and she told me she was considering getting a divorce. But she also said she had something to tell me when I turned 20. I immediately said, 'What are you going to tell me, that I am adopted? I knew it.'

She then started to cry. It was the first time I had ever seen my mother cry. She controlled her emotions as a way of coping with her own demons. She grew up in an abusive home, her father drank, was an alcoholic and abused her and her mother.

I told her that it was okay, I owed everything I had to her and not to worry. She ended up telling me what I knew inside of me to be true, that I was adopted, a bit later. She waited until I had a job

169

so that if I wanted to go out on my own, I was able to support myself.

A close friend of our family, a Jesuit Priest in Almería agreed to meet with me shortly after I got the news. He had seen me grow up from when I was just a toddler. He would just tell me that I was a baby of a mother who couldn't raise me. I wondered if he had some secret to confess to me, but he never said anything, and I respected his silence.

But I wondered, who was my mother? What was she like? So many thoughts race through your mind. Am I the daughter of a rape, of a drug addict, a young, single girl who got pregnant, all these fears, but you don't share it with anyone because you feel shame, but don't know anyone who is in your same shoes and you want the truth but not to cause more sadness to your mother.

So, you try to turn the page and live your life.

Then, in 2010, my father had died and I had already given birth to my own twin boys and happened to read the newspaper *El País* which had an article about Antonio Barroso and his friend Juan Luís Moreno, who claimed they were stolen and bought by installment payments. Best friends as little boys, they grew up together only to find out by a death-bed confession of Antonio's father that yes, they were both bought from the same priest in Zaragoza.

I was shocked!

But was I, a baby like that, was my case similar?

I wrote an email to Antonio and waited with anxiety 3 or 4 days and then he called me. It was the first time I spoke with someone who had experienced similar feelings and concerns as myself. He told me that he had found out everything, all his records had been falsified and asked me about my case. I didn't know what to say, we had only found out about this web, this mafia of baby stealing in 2009 or at the earliest, late 2008. He said to me, 'Inés, there are thousands of mothers bringing flowers to empty graves.'

What if, my mother was one of those mothers? I ended up crying as I spoke to Antonio. He told me there was a lawyer, Enrique Vila, in Valencia, and that he (Antonio) and Vila were going to present a joint criminal complaint of over 260 cases soon to the *Fiscalía's* (Prosecutor General's) office in Madrid.

After my talk with Antonio, I was finally able to start getting my records and my papers. When I reviewed them, I found out that Dr. Eduardo Vela's handwriting is on many of my papers and he is writing that he assisted my birth from a woman who was infertile and never had a baby. That is a complete falsification of an official public document which in Spain is a crime. Antonio looked at my papers and told me that everything I had was falsified and not true.

Once we know everything in my files are false then we formally file the 260, now 261 complaints in Spain in 2011. But those in power in Spain who have no desire to see victims achieve justice know how to play the game to make the odds worse for victims. The *Fiscalía* separates the cases and sends them each to the local area or region where the supposed birth took place originally. This way, it is harder to show these aren't isolated, low-level cases but a true pattern, a mafia at work.

My first complaint was closed by a local Prosecutor. I knew this was just the beginning. I contacted Guillermo Peña, a lawyer who was aggressively filing victim cases in courts across Spain. He told me that I had a strong case and he would re-file it in a more appropriate court. As of today (2018) he is representing over 170 different stolen baby victims. We did this only with the permission of my adoptive mother. (1)

My mother always said she wanted me to find my biological mom, to find my family but out of love, out of not wanting to hurt her, this was a difficult first step for both of us. I told my mother that to file a complaint in court I may have to report her for what she did with Dr. Vela in adopting me illegally. So, if she wanted me to stop the process or my search to tell me and I would stop. But she said, 'Why? What will happen to me?' I told her, 'Nothing probably. You will not go to jail because of your age and the court can order you to pay me compensation but you have done that since I was born, providing for me, so I would not insist.' I looked at her and she was determined for me to get the truth. 'Don't worry,' I said, 'I will.'

Then, she told me everything she knew, how she had volunteered at several different charities and daycares run by nuns because she loved to care for babies. And how our family friend, the Jesuit priest who also knew Dr. Vela, connected them so that, apparently, Vela would facilitate an adoption. My mom also shared how once they were connected, because my mother did not know Vela before, he, Dr. Vela, had told her to simulate a pregnancy by putting pillows under her clothes, and when he had a baby lined up, he would call. And later, he did. He told my adoptive mother and father he had a baby ready to be picked up and not to worry, that he took care of everything. He was, he said, 'giving a gift to my mother for her years of hard work.'

Guillermo and I kept advancing my case and in 2012 my mother and Dr. Vela have an intense confrontation behind closed doors in a court during a deposition. At one point, my mother who had a walking cane, raises it to hit Vela as he denied even knowing who she was, saying he had never seen her before. 'How,' she yelled, 'Can you deny knowing me after you gave me a baby girl as a gift? How?'

But after all of the work, the testimonies, the anxiety and the pain, we are now at a new point for Spain. This is the first time, a case of stolen babies gets this far in court, to the point where now

Dr. Vela will be on trial and will have to answer for what he did, not just in my case but this may open the doors to all the victims he deceived for decades.

Before my mother passed away recently, she and I were watching a news story on Dr. Vela. It was done, I believe, by a French reporter who brought a hidden camera into his San Ramón Clinic before it was shut down. And my mother recognized his wife, Adela, on TV, who was standing behind Vela as the reporter asked him if he had ever given away a baby and he responded that yes, yes, he had done this. He even added, 'She (me) was a gift and that he didn't charge her (my mother). My mother said, 'Inés, you see, he admitted it.' She then said, 'And his wife, that's the woman who took you upstairs and put the baby clothes on you that we bought just before you arrived. She knew.' They all knew."

We paused at this juncture not due to any majestic filmmaking decision but because we heard from the family pet, a cat, we nicknamed *El Rey*. It was apparently, time for dinner and while justice may wait for no man as they say in America, it most certainly must at least pause for *El Rey*.

When we reconvened, we asked Inés what she was feeling at this point, with the trial looming ever so near.

"You know, everybody always asks me how I feel about this upcoming trial of Dr. Vela. The truth?

I feel only shame. Shame, because this shouldn't be the first trial after over 2000 cases are closed, cases with evidence and real victims and real criminals. Each claim by a victim represents real pain and suffering of all the family and the pain of the loss of loved ones and family that will never be reunited. And our politicians continue to talk and make promises but make no real progress and meanwhile, they have been stealing babies and getting away with it for over 60 years."

173

Like Chary and Ascensión, whom you met earlier in this book, Inés also became the president of a local stolen baby association where she lives in an effort to help others like herself. She told us that there are over 130 families just in her smaller area of Murcia searching for loved ones.

"They are waiting for so many of us to die so that this problem will go away. But we will not go away. I know that my case will go down in the darker side of Spain's history with stolen babies but if that is what it takes to finally get to the truth then so be it.

We, all victims, are taking care of things that should be taken care of by the state administration, the judicial system. For me, when I started seeing all of these cases getting no assistance, it was an emotional slap in the face, a shock really, to see how the Spanish Attorney General (Minister of Justice Gallardón) opens an official office as part of the Justice Ministry located in Madrid at *Avenida de la Bolsa, Número 8,* and holds press conferences to tells us all that in this office we will be able to ask for our official documents and records and things will finally get done. But the truth is, when you go there, they tell you, 'Well, we don't have any actual legal ability or standing to take any action on your behalf. We aren't going to look for your baby or child on your behalf, or your true origins, that, you must do yourself.'

So, why do I, why do any of us need such an impotent, sham of an office?

But this is the way they supposedly did something "official" without really doing anything at all. They have not investigated anything, and they provided us with our "own" office, why? What good is it? Who do they think they are fooling?

What is clear is that everyone knows that in this country babies were stolen with impunity. In fact, Felipe González (Former Prime Minister of Spain) knew it. Back in 1987, his administration modified the criminal penal code so that the

174

preamble states that Spain needs to end baby trafficking in our nation. Why didn't he do anything about it then? (2)

They didn't want to take real action then or now.

We have an ongoing case with a father who goes to the Santa Cristina hospital where Sister María worked, who by the way, was on very close terms with Dr. Vela and they would exchange babies to serve their clients. It was like, 'I need a baby,' and they would say, 'Oh, don't worry,' and send the family to Santa Cristina. In this particular case, the adopting father goes there and sees his daughter (the one promised to him) and right next to her is another baby and he says, 'Give that one to me as well, I can take care of both.' And Sister María allegedly said, 'I can't give you this one, it is reserved for a Minister (a politician) who's picking him up soon.'

Where did these children go? Who took them?

They know.

So, yes, I feel shame for my country. It is unbelievable that of all the cases, of all the mothers looking for their babies, that my case is the first to go to trial. My mother spoke up, but many do not, out of fear, out of intimidation, out of being told they are crazy or that bad things will happen to their loved ones if they cause trouble.

But another big piece to this problem is that we have so many Spanish citizens walking around that do not even know they are adopted because so many of the birth records and adoption records were falsified to cover the tracks of the criminals buying and selling babies. There was a pact of silence between the powerful, on both sides of the political aisle in the hope that the past would just be forgotten, and the victims would go away."

We asked Inés how she felt about the impending trial and if she was aware of how she was being viewed by so many victims, as a type of savior for the cause?

"How do I feel? It's difficult, so many emotions. But it is a job I have to do. Eduardo Vela is not going to say, 'Look Inés, I am going to tell you exactly what happened with your mother.' He will never tell me exactly under what circumstances he separated me from the arms of my mother. Maybe, he won't even show up to the trial!

He is a doctor and has many powerful friends and colleagues in the medical profession, they will sign some 'doctor's note' to say he is too feeble or old to take the stand, even though we all know that is false and he retains a sharp and cunning mind. He already placed all his property and wealth in other family member's names and ownership so that if he does get convicted and forced to pay, well, he can plead poverty. Is that the work of some doddering, old man? Certainly not.

How can I stop now that we are so close to having the first stolen baby trial in Spain? I spoke to several jurists who told me it will be very difficult to actually get him sentenced, even with evidence, but he was already investigated for irregularities in his private practice back in 1981, that's why he had to shut that down. But so many crimes for so many years, the justice system wants to put it on someone so why not him? But probably a 'soft sentence,' they don't want to upset him so much that he 'spills the beans,' as they say in English, yes?

But to be clear, if you ask any of us or any mother, 'What do you want? Do you want money? Vengeance? Put the guilty in prison? Or, do you only want to see your baby?' I get goosebumps because I know what we all want, it is to make sure our babies know they were not abandoned, to know they are okay, they are healthy and happy.

When uninformed people go on TV or they intentionally want to discredit us, they need to know, we are not out for material goods. I don't even care if Dr. Vela goes to prison at this point, all

176

I care about is to know the truth. I want to know what happened. Who is my real mother? Where is she? Do I look like her? Think like her?

This is what we think about. This is what we want. Why are they so afraid of us? Because they don't want all the dirty secrets to see the light of day.

Ultimately, no matter what happens to Dr. Vela, our hope is that the attention on this case, on this upcoming trial will be so widespread that victims across Spain will have better chances of having their cases opened or re-opened. Our hope is that prosecutors will not simply say '*archivado*' when there is evidence or falsified records out of perhaps, some fear that they will be made an example of malfeasance or trying to cover-up. But many in power have been doing this for so long maybe this is just a dream or a false hope."

We bid farewell to Inés but only for the moment. We would soon see her again, though, under much different circumstances. The next time would be in Madrid on day one of the trial of Dr. Vela. And it promised to be as chaotic as it would be significant.

Next up, the trial begins in Madrid and we are there to film the events as they unfold.

177

Chapter 9
INÉS MADRIGAL
PART II: The Trial

In the days leading up to the trial of Dr. Vela, the Spanish media, to borrow an American phrase, was in the middle of a feeding frenzy. The local and national news media as well as the talk shows and 'infotainment' shows were all abuzz and atwitter as they posed explosive questions intended to stir the controversy and peak viewer interest. Would the 85-year-old, retired gynecologist even show-up to the trial? Would he, as many victims feared, "play the feeble fool" and fake some ailment in a sly attempt to curry favor and sympathy with the court? Would some "11th hour" negotiation lead to a settlement and spare Vela from taking the stand and being cross-examined?

Adding to the already bubbling drama was the fact that his son-in-law was serving as his lawyer, and he had already signaled the media and the court in preliminary brief court hearings that his father-in-law, his client, the accused, was "not well." In fact, they weren't sure his health could endure this "traumatic experience" of taking the stand. Would the court be open to an indefinite delay?

Meanwhile, the accuser, Inés Madrigal and her lawyer, Guillermo Peña, who was fast gaining a reputation as the "stolen baby victims' lawyer," was also being cautious and careful to tamp down expectations as the trial approached. This was not going to be easy and the judicial system in Spain was complicated, he warned a perhaps, over-eager audience.

Still, as we traveled throughout Spain, interviewing victims at rallies in Sevilla, Valencia, Málaga, Barcelona, and in our meetings with victims in San Sebastián and Bilbao, the mood was

178

cautiously upbeat. Maybe, just maybe, this would be the case, the trial that would finally expose what the powerful, the mafia, had tried to keep secret for decades. They all were careful to say they hoped for the best for Inés, but many were also not shy about noting what a guilty verdict might do to help them advance their own stolen baby cases.

Finally, the first day of the trial was upon us. We made our way to Madrid and were fortunate enough to have been granted full level press access to the event. In practice, this meant we could roam about outside the courtroom filming the massive crowds of victims and supporters assembled just yards away from the court's front door while also being allowed inside to the "press pool." The latter (press pool) allowed us to film the actual trial in real-time on a closed-circuit television monitor. Except for the parties involved, witnesses and immediate family, no one else, save for the judges and attorneys, was allowed inside the courtroom.

Despite day one being held on a work week and it being blazing hot outside, the crowds were lively and vocal as a phalanx of heavily armed Guardia Civil (police) (1) served as a physical barrier between the crowds and the courtroom. There were also several armored vehicles strategically parked to further prevent the crowd from storming the courtroom just in case they were so moved to try.

The media were flying about like a swarm of bees and several of the victims in the crowd wearing brightly colored tee-shirts representing their local stolen baby associations were the honey. Suddenly though, as if an orchestra conductor had given the cue, the crowd began to slowly rise-up as one in body and voice, reaching a crescendo pitch of energy and excitement. Luckily, we were positioned at various vantage points for filming and we captured the moment. It was Inés, she was making her way to the entrance of the court and she was acknowledging the crowd and it seemed as if they were all trying to instill her with all their hopes, pride and strength for what lay ahead as they applauded her and cheered her on.

But just as this moment had reached its apex it shifted suddenly and unmistakably. We spotted a few of the media with their large TV station-style cameras quickly making their way towards an underground parking garage as a black sedan with tinted windows slowly rolled toward its entrance. We sped toward where this car was approaching and soon filmed what had caused the mood of the crowd to change. The car was transporting Dr. Vela and his wife to the court. As he approached many in the crowd which had gathered just above the entrance on both sides began pointing at the car and yelling, hissing and cursing. If, this was a sporting event it was crystal clear who was the home-town hero and who was the visiting villain.

We made our way inside the court facility and by a stroke of luck we nearly bumped into Inés as she was headed into the courtroom to give her testimony and answer questions from a nearly all-female panel of judges. Clearly emotional, she was happy to see us, and we wished her well.

Soon enough the trial began. Inés shared her story and how she came to accuse Dr. Vela of falsification of public records and of facilitating an improper if not illegal adoption of her as a baby. The judges asked her background questions as did Vela's son-in-law turned lawyer. In the Spanish judicial system, the judges, not the attorneys are the dominant truth-seekers and fact-finders as opposed to the lawyers and jurors in American jurisprudence.

The consensus of the gathered journalists and assembled media in the press pool was that Inés came off as clear-headed, calm and determined. And honest. Despite some opponents who attempted to frame her and really all victims as simply advancing some hoax for a hoped-for future "pay-day," this victim at least,

180

came off as merely wanting to know the truth and had evidence to support her claims.

Again, the crowd's mood changed, this time of the gathered press, as the accused, Dr. Vela took the stand. His defense team had chosen to bring him into court in a wheelchair (though he was able to walk just fine) with a sweater draped over his shoulders as he complained he had a chill. He also seemed to have a great deal of trouble speaking much above a whisper even with a microphone set-up at his witness table. As the judges asked him rather basic, establishing questions, it soon became apparent that one of two things had transpired in just a few days since his last public appearance where he seemed quote lucid and vigorous. One, he had suddenly become quite feeble and was struggling with his mental faculties which seemed to elude him even on simple questions, or two, he was playing a role designed to elicit sympathy. In this exchange, for example:

Judge: "Do you recall hiring people at your clinic in San Ramón?"

Vela: "My what? What is this?"

Judge: "Your clinic, you had a private clinic at San Ramón for over 15 years, correct?"

Vela: "I, I don't know. I don't recall."

And so, it went. At one point he was shown documents with his signatures and he claimed to not be able to read the name and later, denied it was his signature. When he was shown side-by-side signatures of documents he had signed over the years on a variety of subjects, which matched exactly the signature in question, he simply reverted back to saying that he didn't know and couldn't say for sure. He complained about the temperature in the courtroom.

At several points he appeared to either fall asleep or briefly lose consciousness, and he seemed to awake with a startle as he

181

breathed into the microphone and grasped for even the simplest of words which seemed to completely elude him. In just a span of 6 minutes alone, by our count, the accused said, "I don't know" or formed these words without actually saying them aloud over 24 times.

Perhaps, the testiest exchange occurred though, between one of the judges and a confidential witness for Dr. Vela. This witness was only allowed to be shown on the court camera from the neck down to protect her anonymity. Despite working alongside Dr. Vela for years this witness did not seem to ever recall any adoption or seeing any babies as described in the court filings. The court did not seem to fully believe her, and the witness became irritable and defensive.

As the court went into a brief recess, we made our way outside and conducted on-the-spot interviews to gauge the crowd's mood and note their expectations. Many wanted to be positive, but the majority felt that Vela would just lie and somehow elude justice.

"He should rot in hell along with Sister María," one victim emphatically told us.

Soon, the trial resumed, though bereft of the fireworks of the opening session. With the day ending, we were informed that questioning had ended and would resume the next day. We once again made our way outside to try and get a glimpse of the participants before they exited the court and protest area for good.

First to exit were the two witnesses for the defense. The media rushed towards them and they answered questions in a defiant and defensive manner. One of the escorts for the first witness attempted to open her car door to transport the witness away and admonished the crowd "To show some respect." Of the many things she could have said, this was probably not the wisest choice. The crowd only became more intense, more passionate and more vocal. Later, when our film crew compared notes, we all

182

shared the same fear at that moment, that the police were about to lose control of the angry crowd.

But, as several cursed at the witness and vented pent-up frustration at what they saw as living embodiments of the web or mafia that had stolen and sold babies and were now helping cover it all up, another witness emerged from the courtroom which triggered even greater emotion from the crowd. This was the confidential witness, the close co-worker of Dr. Vela's, who somehow seemed not to even be aware of any babies being stolen, illegal adoptions or victims. At least not in her 15 or more years of providing medical assistance to the good doctor. The media was skeptical of her stance, to say the least. Mara was able to briefly "interrogate" the witness:

Mara: "So, you never saw any babies being taken?"

Witness: "Never. What are you saying?"

Mara: "You really expect anyone to believe you? All those years at his clinic, and you don't remember anything?"

Witness: "Stop, stop all of these questions."

Again, the tide changed, swiftly and powerfully.

Just as it had when he arrived at the underground garage, the mood shifted as some people who had been perched above the parking garage began yelling that Vela was starting to exit. In just a few seconds, the crowd had enveloped the garage while the police tried desperately to maintain an open lane for the car to exit and reach the access road which led away from the court facilities and crowd.

Exiting in his car though was like slowly facing a moving gauntlet of hostility, anger and resentment. "You bastard," and "May you burn in hell for all eternity" were only some of the sentiments hurled at the car which led Vela away. At one point several pounded at the car, while again, the police physically restrained many from doing worse. Both to the outside of the car and to Vela who sat impassively inside.

As the crowd began to calm down a bit, we again canvassed them and the emotions were raw, the open wounds still very much unhealed. "Justice is only for the powerful not for us," many told us. "Vela will drive away and never return" a victim from Barcelona predicted. (2)

We swung our camera toward the courtroom entrance one last time as Inés Madrigal and her lawyer, Guillermo Peña, approached the crowd. Inés was greeted as a conquering war hero returning to her countrymen and women. The applause, the hugs, the tears were all on display as the crowd seemed to collectively embrace Inés and all she meant to them and all she represented at that moment.

And this was just the first day of the trial!

Before we left the scene, we compared notes with some of the journalists covering the trial, including María José Esteso, whom you will recall we interviewed and chronicled her view in Chapter 7. The consensus was that Dr. Vela had not done much to combat the charges on this first day. We all expected that his team would try some stratagem to delay any type of guilty verdict, which was now looking quite possible.

Soon, we had our answer.

Vela's lawyer requested that the trial be delayed due to his client's suddenly worsening physical condition and overall frailty.

This request was granted.

We made our way in the interim to Valencia to film a private exhumation of a client of Enrique Vila's which turned out to be strange indeed. Not only did this client not find any stolen baby in the coffin they exhumed but what they did find was a skeleton rather neatly preserved in a suit which the Medical Examiner present at the site estimated was well over 125-150 years old.

While we can't say what occurred in this case as the details remain fairly sketchy, we can say with absolute certainty that the visual it represented on our film was, in a word, stunning.

Days later, and with the trial still delayed due to the apparent frailty of the accused, we arranged for an exclusive follow-up interview with Inés Madrigal.

Now that the emotion and anxiety of the initial day of the trial had subsided, we were curious as to how she felt, what her reaction was to the whole spectacle.

With *El Rey* (her beloved cat), perched on top of her sofa, with a sleepy indifference which all cats seem to have innately mastered, we began:

"Incredible. I am very naïve because at first, I thought that at the first day of the trial he, Vela, would not show up. I thought we won't actually have a trial. He is going to be sick or have some accident, something will happen or come up and it won't take place. So, I thanked him when I passed him in the hall of the courtroom before it started. I thanked him for coming, he didn't reply but he looked at me, almost in surprise. I mean, if he doesn't show up there is no trial. And at the end of that first day, his lawyer, his son-in-law, in almost a whisper to the lead Judge, asked her if it was possible for Vela to not come the next day. She told him that, no, he had to show up, he was the accused and he was fine (physically) to be sitting in the court simply answering questions.

The lawyer was of course, preparing the grounds for Vela to not attend afterwards due to his "frailty."

It is a pity too, because when he was excused the second day and the trial delayed, we were not able to show the court by videoconference, the French journalists who had filmed Dr. Vela undercover previously admitting to taking and giving away babies.

So, it was like a dream, and I couldn't believe it (the trial) was really happening on that first day. I was proud of myself and surprised, I guess, because I didn't have any hatred towards him (Vela). It was important for the case for me to stay neutral and calm. It was impressive in the amount of national and international media outlets covering the trial. I have been told that news reporters from Australia, China, Japan, Europe, the USA and your crew, of course, were there and covered the event. That is important as it helps everyone know that here, in Spain, babies were stolen and sold to other families and they tried to cover it up for decades.

But now, we have to see what happens as we are told that Vela was taken to an emergency room after the first day of the trial. But they have not produced any information or documents indicating where he was taken or why. We have informally heard that a close friend of his, a doctor, may have looked at him at his house but it is still unclear.

It is all a lie. Humbug. Hopefully, it will resume again soon."

[Below is a brief transcript of Mara and Greg asking questions to Inés as part of the documentary filming]

Mara: "If it does not resume within 30 days is it true that you have to start the process all over again?"

Inés: "Yes, and that would be awful."

Mara: "Were his responses in court about what you thought they would be?"

Inés: "Yes, Vela's lawyer, as you know is his son-in-law, and he has done his job quite well. He has kept extending the process and delayed the actual trial from starting as long as possible. It would not surprise me if they all hoped he (Vela) would die soon so that his name would not be tarnished, and they already have his wealth as he transferred it all to them to avoid the law."

Greg: "Are you surprised to see him in the courtroom

186

confined to a wheelchair, it seemed that on interviews he gave recently he was able to walk just fine. Is this what many thought he would do, 'play the feeble fool?'"

Inés: "Yes, I was surprised, he does walk fine. A few years ago, when he had the courtroom confrontation with my mother, he was much more agile and strong. It is true he is a bit older now but still, I believe everything was planned to make that image of him as so feeble and to get sympathy.

I don't know if you noticed but when his side asked questions, he was clear, he answered the questions just fine. But when my side, my lawyer (Guillermo) asked him even basic questions or the judges asked him, he couldn't remember, didn't recall anything, was suffering memory lapses, could hardly speak into the microphone. All a game, he played it well.

When he finished giving his statement and declaring (answering the posed questions) his daughter patted him on the back and said, 'Good job Dad, just like we planned.'

To me, it was clear that everything was planned and well-prepared. He is a cunning person who still has clear faculties and knows what he is doing and what he has done over the years. I saw his family shake their heads during the trial, I hope at least they now have some doubt and wonder if maybe, their father did some of these horrible things so many people say he did."

Greg: "Some victims have told us that you are their hero and they look to you to be the face and voice for their cause, while others say, that this is just one case and not worth all the media attention. What do you think?"

Inés: "It is a great responsibility I feel but one I accept. We are preparing to take the case to the Supreme Court in case by some chance he is not found guilty. I am sure his lawyer will keep pushing to have the case prescribed (disposed of, dismissed) and will appeal to the highest court if he is found guilty anyways. What

187

I want to see is our Supreme Court accept my case and all cases of victims so that a final ruling will be made, once and for all.

I want every stolen baby victim to have the opportunity I have had which is to accuse the guilty in court and seek the truth and a remedy."

Mara: "Many stolen baby victims are choosing to not come forward or to not press their claim like you did, why do you think that is so?"

Inés: "There is a lot of fear. The parents fear telling the adopted kids what really happened because they don't want to lose their children or look bad in their eyes. Others, even strangers have told victims they were adopted but when they ask their parents, they may get manipulated, parents cry, say that such accusations are not true or how they are hurt by just the subject being brought up, so many stop there.

But what they don't know is that when an adopted child is supported by the parents and they help each other in the search then the bond between them, the bond of love grows. Just like in my case."

Greg: "What would you say to victims who are afraid to speak up and name names? Some have told us that they fear being sued like Ascensión was, for telling her truth."

Inés: "You must speak up but make sure you are informed of what you can or cannot legally say in public. Ascen spoke out and claimed her aunt, the nun, did crimes, and even though she has so much evidence, she did not legally file a claim beforehand and so was open to being sued for *calumnia*. She made her claims on national television and it was even published in Almería where the nun is a public figure. But what I would say to all victims is this, when you bring a claim to the prosecutor's office you are saying, 'Look, based upon everything I have, everything I know, this is what happened.' You are not just randomly pointing the finger at people and making wild accusations. You are not making things up to get attention. This fear, this silence, goes against the cause, it hurts all victims. And that is what those in power want, they want every victim to be fearful to stay silent, to just go away. And we cannot do this."

Mara: "What final message would you want to share to the audience who may watch this documentary film?"

Inés: "I would say to all, please help us in this struggle. Come forward and share your story as many Americans, it is true, did come to Spain and left with babies. Some knew it was illegal, perhaps, many did not know and trusted the nuns, the priests and the doctors and nurses.

I would also say, share what you discovered while watching this film with many people, tell them to also watch this film because we need to have the world know what happened here, and that it didn't just happen under Franco. There are cases in the 90s even beyond of baby stealing here in Spain and we need to pressure our leaders to open cases and prosecute the guilty and for the church to open their archives and provide the truth to people. Before it is too late."

With *El Rey* still perched above, the King of all he surveyed, we said our good-byes to Inés. In the Epilogue of this book, we share updates to her case and the trial of Dr. Vela as recently as the winter of 2020.

In the next and final chapter, we look more closely at what has become a global epidemic of baby stealing and human trafficking.

Chapter 10
Baby Stealing: A Global Issue

This much is clear-What started out as punishment eventually turned into profit-making.

As you will recall, at the start of this book we laid out the Nazi-inspired, eugenics plan which the Franco regime relied upon to both punish any surviving enemies or suspected sympathizers from the recently ended Spanish Civil War and prevent their offspring from carrying the so-called "red gene" into the next generation. From the outset, victims told us stories of a widespread mafia, comprised of doctors, nurses, nuns, priests and baby-brokers. All of whom were part of a nefarious web or criminal network which took newborn babies from their mothers, sold them to more "suitable families" and then used deception and fraud to cover-up their crimes.

As we pointed out, as did several experts in Chapter 7, like María José Esteso and Franciso González de Tena, when Spain began opening itself up to the west, as part of a commercial initiative to build its economy, this mafia set its sights on even more profit. The result was an expansion in this black-market baby stealing and smuggling. Clients came from all over the world to take babies from Spain during the 1950s and beyond and did so with utter impunity. With the state and church being so closely aligned in this enterprise, this "unholy alliance" operated in unison to steal babies and sell them for illegal adoptions, exploiting a global demand with a supply of newborn Spanish babies. Babies were sold both within Spain and smuggled abroad to places like the USA, Puerto Rico, Colombia, Argentina and throughout Western Europe where the demand was high.

What is also sad but equally clear, is that Spain is far from being the only nation where rampant baby-stealing and selling took place for decades. In fact, this global "baby black market" is a booming, worldwide, illegal business.

It is estimated that there are 35.8 million victims of human trafficking worldwide annually. Of this figure, nearly 70% of these victims are under the age of 18 with estimates ranging between 10-30% of these being between the age of infant/newborn to age four. The average price of a human being these days is about $90 with new victims occurring at a rate of one every 30 seconds globally. The industry of illegal human theft and trafficking whether it be for illegal adoptions, the sex trade or forced labor is huge. The International Labor Organization estimates that forced child labor alone accounts for between $150-200 billion annually, more than the total GDP of 25% of the nations assembled in the United Nations. (1)

United Nations Reports on the Growing Epidemic

The United Nations Regional Information Center (UNRIC) reports that in 2017 there were at least 75,000-100,000 newborn babies stolen just in the European region and then sold to orphanages who then listed them as "abandoned" of "unknown parents" or sold directly to families whose papers were falsified. In many cases, similar to Spain, this was done by the governments of origin where the babies were stolen or by the attendant caregiver with minimal or no oversight.

UNRIC further reports that of the 1.2 million very young children trafficked each year, there is only one person actually convicted of some crime related to this baby theft and sale for every 1,000 babies/young children trafficked or forcibly and involuntarily transported.

So, not only is business booming when it comes to baby and child stealing and trafficking, there also appears to be relatively little risk of personal consequence in participating in this ongoing criminal enterprise.

The United Nations Office on Drugs and Crime (UNDOC) also has sobering news in terms of just who is doing the most active participation. UNDOC reports that 80% of those involved in the illegal human trafficking, theft and sale of babies to young adults are women, with many of those being in the social work and caring profession, including, nurses, doctors, nuns, social workers and orphanage staff. No wonder, that so many of the victims we spoke with felt there must be some 'manual' or 'handbook' that everyone involved uses since their methods are so similar, no matter where in the world it takes place.

At the nation-state level, some nations and regions seem especially vulnerable and at risk. The Non-Governmental Organization (NGO) *Bachpan Bachao Andolan* (Movement to Save the Children) reports that there are over 100,000 Indian babies and children stolen and appropriated away each year or about 15 every hour of every day somewhere in India. It seems that New Dehli is the most openly brazen "baby market" where the activist Bhuwan Ribhu contends that the current "going rate" for a baby is between $4,000 to $6,000 with rates topping out at $8,000, especially, if the destination is Western Europe or the US.

Countries like Serbia and Guatemala continue to be targeted by criminal baby and children stealing networks. Guatemala continues to rank either first or second worldwide for the proportion of its newborn babies expropriated with many illegally adopted to residents of the USA. Meanwhile, Serbia estimates it loses between 20-30 babies every month to the illegal baby trafficking trade.

According to Guatemalan prosecutor Erick Cárdenas, Guatemalan babies and children are stolen both for illegal adoption and for the growing demand for black market organs. In

192

Guatemala, Cárdenas explains that there is a very sophisticated network of doctors, nurses and staffers all collaborating to steal and sell babies internationally. And despite being a party to the 2017 International Convention on Child Trafficking, Guatemala's domestic laws and judicial system are "complex" with "low penalties" in this area of crime.

Due to its state imposed one-child policy, China is a primary exporter of unwanted and abandoned babies, with the bulk of these babies being illegally adopted to US based parents. Recently, Chinese authorities broke up what they say is the world's largest criminal network of baby stealing and selling globally in Eastern China with nearly 500 persons arrested and detained as being part of this enterprise.

During our on-site filming at a stolen baby rally in Sevilla, we were approached by a gentleman from Argentina who told us that he supported the cause because he knew that his country, Argentina, had endured a very similar past.

Indeed. Like Spain, Argentina endured its own horrific baby stealing and illegal, forced adoptions. Just like the Franco regime, the military dictatorship of Argentina during the so-called "Dirty War" of 1976-1983, punished thousands of dissidents with torture, execution or unexplained "disappearance." And just as Franco and Vallejo-Nágera had twisted eugenics to justify its brutality of republican women to eradicate the "red seed," Argentine dictators ordered the systematic separation and theft of babies born to known or suspected "subversives." They claimed this would ensure that a "new generation of subversives would not rise up and threaten their power."

(https://cnn.com/2012/07/05/world/americas/argentina-baby-theft-trial/index.html)

While certainly not the only advocacy group nor representing all victims, the *Abuelas* or Grandmothers of Plaza de Mayo, is an important and significant advocacy and activist organization which has made a real contribution in speaking truth to power. Founded by victims in 1977 to help all victims find their babies and family and to ensure justice, the *Abuelas* have also helped lead the way in helping document and reunite many stolen babies with their families. Since the creation of a national genetic DNA data bank in 1987 to help find the children, 130 of the approximately 500 children appropriated by the Argentinian dictatorship have been reunited with their lost family. In 2011, the *Abuelas* were honored with the Felix Houphouet-Boigney peace prize in Paris, France for their efforts in combatting the Argentinian issue of baby stealing. (http://unesco.org/new/en/member-states/single-view/news/grandmothers_of_the_plaza_de_mayo_receive_felix_houphouet_b/) (5)

Other nations like Ireland who have also suffered through decades of baby stealing, illegal adoptions and even forced infanticide, reflect an even more internecine history with this issue. Dating back to the late 1940s and early 1950s, the Irish experience seems one of deep rooted abusive and exploitative practices in the Catholic Church coupled with another "unholy alliance" of nurses, doctors and orphanages, working closely together to steal and sell babies and then deceive mothers and cover-up the evidence.

The Irish Examiner (news publication) estimates that between 50,000-100,000 Irish babies and children were sexually and physically abused and beaten with thousands of forced and coercive adoptions and outright theft for profit. In Tuam, Ireland alone, nearly 800 babies died at a Catholic run orphanage in the mid-1950s and are buried in a mass, unmarked grave. Other sites like the Sean Ross Mother and Baby Home at Roscrea, Ireland, had a 50% infanticide rate of illegitimate babies born there with one year reaching 60 of 120 babies killed after being born with dozens others sold to the highest bidder [*please see*] (https://irishexaminer.com/viewpoints/columnists/victoria-white/irelands-generation-of-stolen-children-deserve-to-know-who-they-are-248731.html).

As chronicled in the NY Times special report, "The Lost Children," so frequent were the burials of dead babies and children "that the field near the orphanage was completely bare of green grass from digging graves to bury their dead" [*please see in part*] (https://irishexaminer.com/viewpoints/columnists/victoria-white/irelands-generation-of-stolen-children-deserve-to-know-who-they-are-248731.html).

Recently, in part due to continued advocacy and the acclaim and worldwide publicity of the film *Philomena* which documented such brazen abuse, theft and murdering of Irish babies, Pope Francis made an historical pilgrimage to Ireland. There, he offered a formal apology to all victims and their families on behalf of the Catholic Church. The Pope stated that "We ask for forgiveness for those members of the hierarchy (of the church) who didn't take responsibility for this painful situation and who kept quiet." The Pope continued, asking, "May the Lord keep this state of shame and compunction and give us strength, so this never happens again and that there is justice" (https://apnews.com/36b31ae6dfc34cb).

Victims and advocates alike in Spain, point to this formal apology as well as more open cooperation by the church in helping Irish victims find out the truth as the "model" which the Catholic Church should apply to all of Spain as well.

The USA as the Main Consumer of Stolen Babies

Across the Atlantic Ocean, the USA has not just been historically, the world's number one destination of origin of illegal adoptions. It too, has had its own past in participating in this criminal enterprise. Perhaps, its most notorious perpetrator was Ms. Georgia Tann who headed the Tennessee Children's Home

Society between 1924-1950 (http://listverse.com/2018/01/31/10-women-who-stole-other-womens-babies/)

This "Home" was simply a cover for her ongoing criminal network of preying upon single, poor and homeless mothers who she (Tann) would then, through deception, coercion or outright theft, take their baby and sell to the highest bidders in cities like Los Angeles or New York City. She would hire women to portray nurses but who, in reality, were simply acting as brokers to line-up buyers for the stolen babies and falsify the paperwork. Tann would even place ads in newspapers offering help to poor, single mothers. When they answered her ad, she would re-locate them to her Tennessee "Home" and then coordinate the birth and delivery of the baby and subsequent theft and sale. Finally, in 1950, just days after being exposed, Tann died suddenly from cancer. Many observers expressed skepticism, stating they had no idea she (Tann) had ever been sick or ailing a day in her life. (http://listverse.com/2018/01/31/10-women-who-stole-other-womens-babies/) (2)

Despite this historical and contemporary exploitation and human trafficking of babies and children worldwide it is also not as if there is no international body of laws in place to prevent and punish these crimes. It just seems such laws are willfully ignored.

The International Laws Against Illegal Abduction and Adoption of Children

Dating back to 1924 with the Geneva Declaration of the Rights of the Child, the 1933 Hague Convention on the Protection of Children and Cooperation in Respect of Inter-Country Adoptions and the 1948 Universal Declaration of Human Rights as well as the 1958 Declaration of the Rights of the Child, the international community has recognized that at least from an aspirational perspective, protecting the rights and safety of all children should be a top priority for a civilized world. However, declaring something as vital or even universally recognized is not the same as eliminating the threat to the very existence of what is being universally recognized. If not, then aspirational declarations would simply be statements of reality. Which, sadly, they are not. (https://ohchr.org/en/professionalinterest/pages/crc.aspx).

In 1980 world leaders attempted to strengthen this protection through the 1980 Hague Convention on Civil Aspects of International Child Abduction. Signed by 99 nations, this Convention called for the prompt return of stolen babies to their biological parent(s) as well as the need to combat known cases of illegal parental child abduction in cases of custodial rights conflict. This Convention also attempted to harmonize the domestic laws of its signatory nations to provide more uniformity and certainty against crimes against children. It was at least partially credited in helping to stiffen penalties against a rather extensive and profitable baby-stealing and trafficking network uncovered by Italian police in 1984 in Marsala, Italy (https://hcch.net/en/instruments/conventions/specialised-sections/child-abduction).

The United Nations Convention on the Rights of the Child

However, the main legal treaty which attempts to address the very broad range of economic, criminal, political, civil, cultural and social issues surrounding the theft of babies and children and subsequent sale and exploitation by others is the United Nations Convention on the Rights of the Child (UNCORC). This was adopted in 1989 and is now signed and ratified by all UN Member-State nations except for Somalia, the South Sudan and the United States (https://ohchr.org/en/professionalinterest/pages/crc.aspx).

The UNCORC, legally binding on all its signatories, applies to every child under the age of 18 (or the age of majority of the signatory state if lower) [Article I] and requires that "in all actions concerning children the best interests of the child shall be the

197

primary consideration" and further, "that all states ensure the child such protection and care as is necessary for his or her well-being." [article 3] (https://ohchr.org/en/professionalinterest/pages/).

Perhaps, most relevant to baby-stealing, the UNCORC states in Article 7 and 8 that, "Every child has the right to be registered immediately after birth and to have a name, the right to acquire a nationality and to preserve his or her identity, and, as far as possible, the right to know and be cared for by her or his natural, birth parents.

Article 35 of the UNCORC urges that national authorities take any and all measures to "protect children against abduction, or sale of children or trafficking in children," while Article 34 urges prevention of "all forms of sexual exploitation and abuse of children" (https://ohchr.org/en/professionalinterest/pages).

However, the problem remains and according to some experts shows signs of strengthening not weakening. Recently, the European Commission on Human Rights stated that it (the EC) "opposes the current transformation of international adoptions into nothing short of a baby market and roundly condemns the continued widespread, falsification of parental documents by many nations of origin and destination" (https://ohchr.org/EN/Issues/Children/Pages/Illegaladoptions.asp x).

The Special Commission on Human Rights of the Child (EC) called for a "total prohibition on private and independent adoptions," noting that the continued rise of non-regulated and private adoptions and in some cases (UK-Ireland) of even accredited agency illegal participation is "proving to be resistant to elimination and continues to be destructive and corrosive." (https://ohchr.org/Documents/Issues/Children/Illegaladoptions/St atement.pdf).

Do International Laws Work?

One of the recurring themes we heard during our filming in Spain was that besides Spain needing to do something to fully address baby stealing and make things right for all its victims, there must also be a much more concerted effort from the international community to leverage or pressure nations like Spain to take aggressive action.

But how effective are international calls for prohibitions on illegal adoptions or even worldwide condemnation of nation-state atrocities and human rights violations like baby stealing for profit?

In other words, without specific sanctions or rewards, do nations like Spain even pay attention to such global pleas, however heartfelt and impassioned they may be?

The reality so far, seems to be that for every Argentina, arguably, an example of justice prevailing despite a nearly forty-year-old struggle, there remains nations like Spain. Nations which seem to continue to largely reject or at least adamantly resist such international calls to solve its domestic problem of baby-stealing of an estimated 300,000 or more of its own citizens.

Spain's Refusal to Embrace International Recommendations

Between 2014-2018, the Members of the European Parliament Committee in Petitions, in response to a number of petitions from individuals and organizations to look into the continued issue of *bebés robados* (stolen babies) of Spain, formed several working groups. They then traveled directly to Spain to gather facts, interview witnesses and officials and to hear and review alleged crimes. In addition, the United Nations Working Group on Enforced and Involuntary Disappearances and the Special Rapporteur on the Promotion of Truth, Justice, Reparation and Guarantees of Non-Recurrence along with the MEP Committee on Petitions Chairwoman Jude-Kirton Darling, have all urged Spain to address this continuing problem. Closer to home, activists like Soledad Luque also urge Spanish leaders of all political stripes to do the right thing and cooperate and uphold their international human rights obligations.

In part, these and other international organizations, leaders and advocates all continue to urge Spain to create a national DNA bank (similar to Argentina) to help locate and reunite missing children (now adults) with surviving members of their biological family. The United Nations Committee on Enforced Disappearances also urged Spain to adopt the provisions of the International Convention for the Protection of All Persons (including children and babies) from enforced disappearance into their own domestic law and urged them to do so at once (http://europarl.europa.eu/news/en/press-room/).

To date, Spain has refused to adopt either the provisions of the International Convention noted above or the creation of a national DNA bank. Currently, if a victim has suspicions about their own biological origin and wishes to search for matching DNA family members he or she must do so only through privately owned and operated DNA companies in Spain, of which the primary one is owned and operated by members of Opus Dei.

Consequently, many victims have stated their skepticism and distrust of the possible DNA findings at this or other privately-run Spanish companies. As a result, many victims are left to pursue oftentimes more expensive and inconvenient paths outside of Spain as far as DNA possible matching. Not having a centralized DNA bank in Spain to search for most probable "hits" makes the process like "searching for a DNA needle in a haystack." (3)

The European Parliament Again Urges Spain to Act

In 2018 the EP Committee on Petitions, noting the relative lack of formal effort of the Spanish government to respond to

200

previous committee recommendations once again called upon Spain to address this problem by doing the following:

1. Create a national DNA bank to facilitate identity checks and possible matches and to offer free DNA tests for alleged victims

2. Appoint a special public prosecutor at a national level dedicated to investigating and prosecuting all alleged baby abductions and illegal adoptions

3. Take steps necessary to ensure full access to all civil registries, records, hospital birth registers and church archives to all alleged victims

4. Provide funding for psychological and legal support and other related assistance for alleged victims (http://europarl.europa.eu/news/en/press-room/ 20171121IPR88505/stolen-babies-meps-urge-spain-to-solve-all-alleged-cases).

However, despite such Spanish officials as the Minister of Justice Rafael Catalá (2016) admitting that this (stolen baby victims and their search) "is a genuine personal and social drama" and reiterating the government's commitment to cooperate with the world community to open access to information and investigations, none of the Committee recommendations and urgings have, to date, been fully adopted by Spain (https://elpais.com/elpais/2017/06/07/inenglish/1496830014_713 027.html).

In the film, the Chairwoman of this important Committee (EP Committee on Petitions) spoke with us and shared the frustration of many victims with this slow process and almost, non-existent willingness by Spain to take action. Chairwoman Jude Kirton-Darling (UK) made the analogy that 'many victims feel like they are a political football, being kicked back and forth by politicians but never scoring that goal, never achieving true justice."

She makes a vital point. Only during the years of the PSOE (Socialist Workers Party of Spain) Zapatero Administration (2004-2010) did Spain, even modestly move towards addressing the *bebés robados* issue. Alleged victims of baby stealing were permitted to pursue judicial and private exhumation orders under the broad umbrella of Historical Memory reform related to victims of the Spanish Civil War. Additionally, some largely symbolic initiatives were promulgated which recognized in a legally non-binding way alleged stolen baby victims and their struggle for justice.

However, actual funding for tangible items like the above-mentioned national DNA bank or subsidized investigations and prosecutions remain just that, largely symbolic. Until or if, the Amnesty Law of 1977 is rescinded or at least reformed, activists like María Garzón remain highly skeptical that any real investigations or trials ending in convictions for crimes during the Franco era will ever be a reality. Many remain convinced that the Spanish officials have no real desire to take such legislative action which the international community continues to urge them to take. (http://europarl.europa.eu/cmsdata/137380/1141947EN)

Certainly, for many victims of baby theft and forced adoption, truth and justice continue to remain as elusive as stopping the day from becoming night. In Spain, it becomes increasingly clear that only through massive political change and action can this nightmare end. Recently, with the change of government at the national level and the ascendancy once again of the PSOE party after years of nearly uninterrupted dominance by the ultra-right-wing PP leadership, some victims are hopeful that reforms will come. They are optimistic that these will help them finally discover their own truth and achieve justice.

Many others though, remain highly doubtful. They see the clock continuing to tick and believe the Government is simply delaying doing anything as long as possible in the hopes that many victims will not live long enough to continue the fight. Despite his own death in 1975, the dictator Franco continues to cast a large shadow of doubt and fear over many victims who know that the roots of his dictatorship continue to run deep. Especially, among the ultra-conservative, far-right leaders, who are seen as the contemporary descendants of Francoism. Change, if it comes at all to Spain, will not be easy or swift.

Some Good News on the Horizon

Globally, the good news seems to be a growing awareness and recognition of the many atrocities committed against babies and children and the need to develop even greater worldwide protections for this vulnerable population. Whatever the reason, be it, ideological, political or just plain greed, these immoral and illegal acts are facing a growing body of international law and case holdings which condemns such behavior and seeks to strengthen sanctions against it.

However, sadly, a basic principle of economics persists. Where there is a demand, somewhere, there will be a supply to meet that demand. And some agreed upon price point will occur and a transaction will take place. Only when there is such an overwhelming disincentive for this exchange to occur will such a criminal enterprise cease to exist.

As Pope Francis reminds us all, "Never forgetting the shame that such acts against the most vulnerable among us took place is the first step to a lasting solution." (4)

But victims want to do more than just never forget. They want to take that step. Basic human rights and fairness demands they not take that step alone. Spain must embrace these victims, admit the decades of wrongdoing and confront its dark past of baby stealing and systemic fraud and deception. Only by confronting its past, holding the guilty accountable and clearing the path of

203

unnecessary obstacles for those who search, will all victims, all *bebés robados* and their loved ones, finally have a fair chance at finding truth, justice and reconciliation. Before it's too late.

Epilogue

When we first started this journey together in the *Prologue*, we shared how many victims describe the baby-stealing network that plagued Spain for decades as simply, the Mafia. Then and now, many victims are hesitant to speak out in public about their plight. They fear governmental retaliation by those in power who seek to suppress the truth and keep the secrets of Spain's dark past dead and buried. They know all-too well what victims like **Ascensión** have endured for running afoul of Spain's laws which seem patently designed to protect the powerful rather than assist those in need, whether armed with evidence or not.

Some stolen baby victims have stopped speaking out about crimes that were done to them not out of fear but out of distrust and disbelief. They simply don't trust their government, judges, prosecutors, politicians, doctors, nurses, nuns and priests to simply do the right thing. They have learned the hard way over the years that powerful institutions like the Catholic Church in Spain and the Vatican seem to feel it has more to lose by coming clean and opening its archived adoption and birth records than it has to gain in helping so many victims who seek loved ones and their true ancestry. They don't believe things will ever change.

So, some have simply stopped. And with that their hope has faded if not disappeared altogether.

Too many opened and closed cases despite evidence to the contrary, too many falsified documents that cleverly covered-up crimes and made it nearly impossible to track down the truth. Too many tears shed and too many promises made and promises broken. Too many years of unanswered prayers.

One of the most recurring sentiments that we kept hearing as we filmed was the widespread belief that those in power in Spain, many of whom are the political and biological descendants of Francoism, are simply determined to "wait out" victims until they simply are too old to fight anymore. "They want us to simply go away, die off, so we will never know the truth or be reunited with loved ones," many victims told us.

Those in power, be they elected officials whom we interviewed or *fiscalía* (prosecutors) and judges who refused to comment on the record, both share a certain world view when it comes to stolen baby victims. It goes something like this; "Our hands are tied. The Amnesty law prevents us from prosecuting crimes of the past. There is no funding to do what victims want like establishing a national DNA laboratory. It is not our fault."

Making matters worse, as the number of stolen baby victims who came forward grew, so did certain "experts" who attempted to dismiss them all as merely engaging in some type of hoax, or who only were aimed at getting money.

Of course, nothing could be further from the truth. If there was another widespread sentiment shared by victims we interviewed on and off-camera, it was an utter disregard for and disinterest in being given any compensation for their loss. What they seek is not material goods or money. They simply yearn for what so many of us take for granted every day. The simple touch, the closeness, the nearness of, loved ones. The ability to say "I love you" to a mother, a father, a sister, a brother, a daughter, a son.

For many, like **Lidia**, this longing, this prolonged emptiness, is unbearable.

Yet, still, many persist.

And for some, this persistence, even in the face of incredible odds, is paying off.

DNA testing and the increased accuracy and ease of access which such technology represents has allowed some to find their true ancestry and be reunited with family members they never knew, never could have dreamed, existed.

You will recall in Chapter Three how **Mercedes** and her daughter **María José**, for example, were confirmed as mother and daughter through DNA matching despite what Mercedes alleges was outright fraud by a genetics lab in Spain. And this is far from being the only case where victims allege fraud and deception by domestic, Spanish DNA labs.

The lesson here for many victims is not to submit to or rely on DNA testing in Spain but to seek out private DNA laboratories abroad. Victims remain convinced that the DNA laboratories in Spain, especially the large ones run by Opus Dei or affiliated with the church are not reliable or trustworthy. There are too many instances like Mercedes, who was wrongly told her tests were negative or others who were told there were no matches yet when they tried other laboratories abroad, like *23andMe*, they found matches. "It's no coincidence," one victim told us, "This is just another way to keep the truth hidden."

International pressure from organizations like the United Nations or the European Parliament and its working groups and committees led by chairpersons like **Jude Kirton-Darling** (UK) remain an important tool to try and convince Spain to fully address their stolen baby victim problem. This, these groups say, can be accomplished, by both honoring its current international commitments as well as reforming its domestic laws to help all victims find the truth they seek. Establishing a specialized investigative unit with specialized police, prosecutors, investigators and psychiatrists as other nations with similar issues have done, can certainly be done as well in Spain.

But the political will must exist. The desire to confront its own dark past and embrace the truth, wherever that truth may lead, must exist.

So far, Spain has, at best, shown an uneven willingness to do what is just and fair.

Of course, as has been made clear in this book, Spain is far from being alone in its continued determination to keep secrets of its past hidden.

Recently, in the late summer (August 31st) of 2019, several members of stolen baby associations mentioned in this book, including **Lidia and Marga** (Sevilla and Bilbao) met with Pope Francis at the Vatican in Rome. This marked the first time that the Pope agreed to meet with a delegation from Spain representing stolen baby victims. Clearly, this was seen by victims as a step forward on behalf of the Catholic Church. They exhorted the Pope to allow the archived church records of adoptions and births to be opened and accessed by victims seeking the truth, both in Rome and throughout Spain.

Reportedly, he agreed to do what he could and to support them in their cause.

However, like other times when victims met with Bishops and other church leaders who made similar promises of support, so far, no tangible action has occurred.

Yet, still, many persist. With or without the help of those in power.

Ascensión continues to fight to stay out of prison for what she sees as simply telling the truth in her case. A telling element, her case continues to be contemplated on apparent damage done to a powerful nun (her aunt) whom she claims coordinated her illegal adoption yet the underlying merit of what Ascen claims does not seem to be challenged or disputed.

In Spain, it seems when the truth hurts those in power that may be the real crime.

Clara continues to petition to have the court nullify the original adoption of her daughter which Clara asserts was a conspiracy. A conspiracy coordinated by the judge who had legal custody over her (Clara) as a minor and is now the Minister of Defense of Spain, her alleged social worker, who ended up taking possession of her baby and a lawyer who it seems was working against Clara's interests.

Though the court recently denied her petition in late 2019, Clara stated her commitment to appealing the decision in early 2020.

Her relationship with her daughter Marina, whom she was reunited with not too long ago, has been strained by the stress of these proceedings and claims.

Ted, who was able to find his biological sister in Spain is still committed to finding out the truth of his own ancestral parents and birth, yet it seems his mother took those secrets with her to her grave.

Meanwhile, Dr. Eduardo Vela, whom you will recall, when we last discussed him, was asking for his trial to be delayed due to undisclosed health concerns, never did return to court. And while he never produced required documentation for his absence, he was nevertheless, tried, found guilty and convicted in absentia. However, the court also ruled that no penalty would be assessed, nor any incarceration be imposed for having been found guilty of, among other things: falsifying public records, coordinating illegal adoptions and lying under oath.

The reason the court gave was that the statute of limitations for bringing such an allegation against the accused had expired. The court rejected what seemed like a commonsense argument from Inés' lawyer which essentially was, how could she bring a claim against Dr. Vela until or if, she had some reason to believe she was adopted, and he had been involved?

The judiciary in Spain apparently is not driven by commonsense.

Inés and her lawyer plan to appeal the decision in the national tribunal supreme court. As Inés puts it, "Not so much for this case but for all victims who should not be denied justice because they would be expected to do the impossible- somehow file a claim even before they realize they were adopted or have evidence to implicate anyone in specific."

Perhaps, nature stepped in where impotent judges merely stepped aside. On October 21st, 2019, not long after he was found guilty, Dr. Vela died, surrounded by family. A fate which many victims will be denied at their final hour of passing.

As for Inés, while she was never able to find any biological family through any Spanish DNA labs, using the USA-based, *23andMe* lab, she was able to identify three biological brothers and a sister on her first try. Ironically, her family had been searching for their long-lost sister as well, but again, for some reason, perhaps several, they were told there were no such matches in using labs based in Spain. Though, Inés' biological mother died in 2013 at the age of 73, Inés and her newly discovered siblings continue to get to know each other and marvel at their own similarities, physical and emotional.

As for Enrique, he continues to search for his own biological mother, and works on behalf of victims to help facilitate reunions and recently argued the first stolen baby victim case in front of the UN Committee on the Rights of the Child in Geneva. He also continues to work closely with us on projects like this book and future films and appears on numerous television shows in Spain to help raise awareness of this issue throughout Spain and beyond. "It is," as he puts it, "Not something I ever planned on but now, not something I could ever imagine not doing."

And so, in a sense, we have now come full circle.

It has been said that evil flourishes when good men and women choose to do nothing.

We thank you for caring enough to read this book. You are now among the good men and women of this world who are at least armed with the truth about the stolen baby victims of Spain.

What, if anything, you decide to do next with this knowledge may well make a difference to victims everywhere.

For more information about stolen babies of Spain and ways you can help, please visit *www.stolenbabiesofspain.com*.

Truth. Justice. And Reconciliation.

Glossary

Note: English terms are in normal script, Spanish terms are italicized.

ABRA- Asociación Bebés Robados de Andalucía- A stolen baby association in the Andalusian region (south) of Spain.

Abuelas de Plaza de Mayo (Argentina)- Common usage term for a group of grandmothers who all suffered loss of family due to a kidnapping and disappearance campaign by the Argentinian regime in the late 1970s and 1980s and, along with advocacy groups helped find many though not all of these "stolen" babies.

A las bravas- A slang term in Spanish which roughly translates to "on my own."

Amnesty Law of 1977- A domestic, compromise law passed by both the right and left political coalitions of Spain as a means to allow a smoother transition from the Franco regime into a fledgling democracy, though, it provided immunity for prosecution of criminal acts committed prior to this date as it related to issues like stolen baby victims or post-civil war related crimes against avowed enemies or opponents of Franco. Many critics argue that international treaties signed by Spain supersede any such domestic law when it comes to crimes against humanity and children.

ANADIR- Asociación Nacional de Afectados por Adopciones Irregulares (National Association of People Affected by Irregular Adoptions).

ANDAS- Asociación Nacional del Derecho a Saber (National Association of the Right to Know).

Antonio Vallejo-Nágera- A military psychiatrist whose theories on race, eugenics and Nazi-inspired social control were influential in the implementation of public policies post-Spanish

Civil War by the Franco regime, aimed at control, elimination of dissidence and suppression of contrary thought and action.

Archivado- Literally "archived," this refers to the frequently quick and summary decision by prosecutors in Spain to file away or permanently close cases or claims that have been brought for investigation by stolen baby victims or their family.

Asociación Víctimas de Alicante- A stolen baby victims association in Alicante, Spain.

Asociación Sevilla Bebés Robados- A stolen baby association in Sevilla, Spain.

Auxilio Social- Re-instated by executive decree shortly after the civil war, these were centers for children and young adults who had been displaced, abandoned or orphaned. Many survivors of these *Auxilios* tell of horrible conditions, brutality and abuse by those who ran these centers, often priests.

AVA- Asociación Víctimas de Alicante.

A Young Mother in Franco's Prisons- A book based on a diary kept by Pilar Fidalgo, a young mother who survived being held prisoner during the Civil War.

Baby Cabbies- Slang for taxi-cab drivers who were paid to transport stolen babies by their cabs.

Baby Chalets- Slang for undisclosed homes where many single, young, pregnant women were kept until the time of their delivery, often under the control of the church and on-site nuns.

Bebés Robados- Stolen Babies.

Bocadillos- Sandwiches.

Calumnia- A Spanish law that provides sanctions and possible jail-time on anyone who is judged to have publicly defamed or slandered another through what is said, or allegations made prior to filing a formal charge. Even having evidence to substantiate one's public claim alone, is not a sufficient defense. Unlike the American laws which provide a more generous zone of

213

public free speech especially against or towards a public or famous figure, the Spanish law of *calumnia* is quite restrictive.

Casa Cuna- Cradle home, a place where pregnant single women were brought by family members to hide their pregnancy and have the baby.

Inclusa- Home for abandoned children, unwanted babies were brought here to be given up for adoption, but it is believed that it acted as a "baby laundering" center where adoptions of stolen babies were falsely made to appear as legal adoptions.

Cuerpo de Divulgación- Body of full disclosure, in practice, the strict monitoring and oversight of women in society by groups like the *Sección Femenina de la Falange*, to ensure full compliance with Francoist law and policy.

Daughters of Charity- One of the more well-known charitable organizations comprised of nuns, many of whom worked or volunteered at clinics where it is alleged that many babies went missing, disappeared, or were stolen and later sold.

Denounce- A legal term which means to prove, normally in court, that an accuser or claimant is making falsehoods or knowingly defaming another.

Diputación de Aragón- Aragón County Council.

DNA Testing- A process where someone provides a DNA sample and then reviews results to see if there are any matches within the database or relatives/ancestry the one doing the testing can discover.

DNI- *Documento Nacional de Identidad*, is the Spanish National Identity Card first created in 1944 during the Franco dictatorship. It's a mandatory document needed by every citizen.

Dr. Eduardo Vela- A retired gynecologist in Spain, who was alleged to have coordinated hundreds, even thousands of illegal adoptions, outright thefts of babies and falsified public documents. He was convicted, though did not end up serving time for allegations of fraud and public document falsification brought against him by his accuser, Inés Madrigal, in the summer of 2018. Vela died shortly after his formal conviction.

El Caudillo- The Warlord, a nickname given to the former dictator of Spain, Franco.

El País- The Nation, the name of a national newspaper and now a hard-copy and digital publication.

El Rey- Literally, the King, a nickname given by the SBOS film crew to a certain feline.

Encounter- A term used by many victims to describe a reunion of long-lost relatives or a meeting for the first time.

European Parliament Committee on Petitions- A permanent Committee which has produced several working reports on the issue of stolen babies in Spain and published several recommendations and suggestions as how Spain can best address this problem. To date, Spain has, at least officially, largely ignored these recommendations.

España es diferente- Spain is Different. A marketing and tourism slogan adopted by Spain to try and showcase its diversity as a travel destination spot.

Eugenic Racism- A theory and public policy which attempts to develop and advance one race over all others through controlled genetics and reproduction.

Exhumations- Public or private digging up of graves or coffins in order to confirm or reject the existence of, or remains of, someone who was or is still buried in the spot being dug up.

Falange- (*Sección Femenina de la Falange*)- A far-right, nationalist ideological group which reached its peak during the assumption of power of Franco and shortly after the Spanish Civil War. The *Sección Femenina de la Falange*, was a sub-group which focused on ensuring loyalty and policy implementation by women of all ages in post-war Spain.

False Baby- (false son)- A baby whose official papers have been forged or falsified to make it appear as though the baby is indeed a natural born offspring of the parents of record when this is not actually true.

Felipe González- Former prime minister of Spain, 1982-1996, a Socialist Worker's Party member (PSOE).

Fiscalía- (*Fiscal General*)- A prosecutor or national prosecutor, similar to the District Attorney or Attorney General of the USA.

Francisco Franco- Former General of the Nationalist forces during the Spanish Civil War, and dictator of Spain between 1939-1975.

Francisco González de Tena- A sociologist and author in contemporary Spain.

Generalitat de Catalunya- The government of Catalonia.

Geneva Declaration of the Rights of the Child- is an international document promoting child rights.

Guardia Civil- A military police force of Spain. The oldest law enforcement agency in the country. See Chapter 9 end notes.

Guillermo Peña- A lawyer who specializes in representing stolen baby victims, he represented Inés Madrigal in the trial of Dr. Vela.

Hija de puta- The daughter of a bitch, an insult to demean a girl or woman whose ancestry is in question or who was adopted.

Historical Memory Act- Legislation passed under prime minister Zapatero (2004-2011) which provided for public resources and programs to formally teach, educate and preserve events, figures and acts of those who suffered persecution during and after the Spanish Civil War, stolen baby victims along with civil war family of victims could also file for and be granted judicial orders to hold public exhumations.

Inclusa- A clinic for babies in Madrid where both Raquel and Magaly spent time as babies and both were documented at the *Inclusa* as abandoned though both dispute this assertion.

José Luis Rodríguez Zapatero- A former prime minister of Spain, 2004-2011, a Socialist Worker's Party member (PSOE).

José María Aznar- A former prime minister of Spain, 1996-2004, a conservative Popular Party member (PP).

Jude Kirton-Darling- A Member of the European Parliament (UK) who serves as the Chairperson of the Committee on Petitions which conducted several Working Group trips to Spain as regards the overall problem of stolen baby victims.

King's Day- January 6th, a day where children in Spain receive presents to commemorate the Three King's or 'Wise Men' who marked the birth of Christ.

La Prisión de Madres Lactantes- A prison for pregnant women and new mothers.

Mafia- A term which many victims use to describe a criminal network or secret organization of many individuals, many in powerful positions, who were (and still are) part of stealing babies and selling them and/or facilitating illegal adoptions without the knowledge or consent of the biological mother/parents.

Manuel García Escobar, aka, **Manolo Escobar**- A popular Andalusian singer and actor, 1931-2013.

María José Esteso- An investigative journalist and author on the subject of stolen babies in Spain.

Mariano Rajoy- A former prime minister of Spain, 2011-2018, a conservative member of the PP (*Partido Popular*).

Marked- A term used to denote someone who has been shamed or ostracized by society for some past real or alleged "sin," whether by their own doing or for events/circumstances beyond their control.

Master Aryan Race- A term used to describe a policy goal during Nazi Germany in which only the "best" or superior citizens would be developed and nurtured while all others seen as less fit or inferior would gradually die-off or be eliminated.

Mentira- A lie, a falsehood.

Mother Superior- A head nun or one who is in charge

MyHeritage- A USA based DNA testing and analysis facility.

Nationalists- The political party of affiliation by followers of Franco, ultra-conservative in ideology.

Nazi Eugenics- A theory of genetics designed to produce only the fittest or most able to implement the Nazi plan of domination and control.

Nazi Eugenecists- Genetic scientists and theoreticians who worked on behalf of the Nazi party.

Neodiagnostica- A DNA testing laboratory in Spain

Nicho- A small, enclosed space where the dead are buried, usually this is part of many buried and is above-ground.

O'Donnell- A slang for the Santa Cristina hospital, so named for the street (O'Donnell) this hospital is located.

Opus Dei- A devout and orthodox Catholic following and sect within the Catholic Church, victims believe that members of Opus Dei, in their desire to protect the church, have and continue to work against victims and their search for the truth, especially in persuading the church to open its archived adoption and birth records in their possession.

Pablo Rosser- A historian and author with the Alicante government.

Patronato de Protección de la Mujer- Centers for young girls and women, while the stated mission was to protect often abused, impoverished women, survivors often tell stories of actual abuse at such centers.

218

Pedro Sánchez- Current prime minister of Spain (2018-) a member of the Spanish Socialist Worker's Party, *Partido Socialista Obreo Español* (PSOE).

Pilar Fidalgo- A survivor of Franco's Prisons and author of a book chronicling her experience while incarcerated.

Pilar Primo de Rivera- Sister of the founder of the Falange in Spain (José Antonio Primo de Rivera), and head of the *Sección Femenina de la Falange* under Franco. Their father was Miguel Primo de Rivera, a former dictator of Spain (1923-1930).

Plead the 5th- Slang for invoking one's legal right to not answer questions which may tend to criminally incriminate someone.

Prescription- Similar to a finding that the statute of limitations has expired or one can no longer file or advance a charge.

Purgando el Comunismo- A process of purging communism, usually consisted of humiliating, painful, sometimes lethal, abuse and torture (often of women) thought to be disloyal to Franco.

Putas, rojas, feas y peladas- Insults and offensive, demeaning names hurled at Republican women or those thought to be disloyal to Franco.

Red Beast- A slang term used to describe anyone or a group of people who believed in or actively supported socialism or communism.

Red Gene- A theory that those disloyal to Franco carried within their DNA, a so-called red gene or genetic pre-disposition to communism, by killing adults who carried this gene or at least by stealing their off-spring and not allowing their 'red' parents to raise them, it was believed that this 'red gene' could then die-off or be eliminated in future generations.

Republicans- Opposition to Franco's Nationalists, seen as more liberal or progressive, ideologically.

219

Ruth Appleby- A stolen baby victim, of English heritage (UK), who alleges her baby, who was born in La Coruña, Spain, was stolen and sold, her case was heard at the high court in Europe.

Santa Cristina- A hospital/clinic in Madrid, alleged to have facilitated hundreds if not thousands of illegal adoptions and theft of babies over several decades.

Second Republic of Spain- A progressive, leftist run government in Spain (1931-1939) which passed numerous reforms, several of which aimed at increasing legal rights to women and reducing the power of the Catholic Church.

Secreto Sumario- By governmental order, an area which the public is not allowed to enter or to view, this was applied and still is to exhumations being conducted in Spain.

Sor María Gómez Valbuena- A nun (sister) who worked at the notorious Santa Cristina (O'Donnell) clinic and was indicted for crimes related to illegal adoptions and baby thefts, she died within days of being formally indicted.

Sor Pura- A nun (sister) who was alleged to have facilitated hundreds if not thousands of illegal adoptions and thefts of babies.

SOS Stolen Babies of Cádiz- A stolen baby victim association in Cádiz, Spain.

Spanish Civil War 1936-39- A civil war between the citizens of the legal government of the Spanish Second Republic (Republicans) and the followers of the military coup d'etat (Nationalists) for control of Spain.

Statute of Limitations- A legal period of time when a claimant or victim can formally bring a charge.

Stolen Baby Corridors- A term used to describe routes or areas where stolen babies were transported from one area to another.

Subnormales- Literally 'subnormal,' a derisive term used to imply that someone is less human than normal.

Telenovela- A term used to describe often dramatic television operas or shows based on popular, romantic books or short novels.

The Lost Children of Tuam- A long piece published by the NY Times which chronicles the lost or stolen children in Ireland due to illegal adoptions, theft of babies or children, or outright murdering of such orphaned, lost or abandoned children.

Truth. Justice. Reconciliation- A slogan used by many victims to state their mission or why they search.

Tu Casa- Your House, the name of an organization in Carabanchel (Spain) for single, young, pregnant women. Victims allege that such places merely ensured healthy deliveries so as to then ensure successful, illegal sales of these babies to buyers. Sor Pura was in charge of this organization.

Universidad Nacional Autónoma de México **(UNAM)-** The National Autonomous University of Mexico, located in Mexico City is the oldest in North America (founded in 1551).

Valle de los Caídos- A memorial to the former dictator Franco, his Nationalist supporters and the church, this large edifice was built by forced labor of the vanquished Republican survivors after the Spanish Civil War and has been supported in large part by public tax dollars. It housed the coffin of Francisco Franco until October 24th, 2019 when, after much controversy, it was finally exhumed and moved alongside his wife, Carmen Polo, to El Pardo cemetery in Madrid.

Walks of Shame- So called public walks of humiliation of known or suspected female Republican loyalists or simply single, unmarried women who were accused of being immoral, suspects were stripped naked and forced to walk in front of fellow neighbors and citizens as part of a process to purge their inherent "evil."

Weimar Republic- A progressive, socially liberal period of time in Germany just prior to the Nazi take-over.

23andMe- A USA based DNA testing lab and facility.

300+- The number of interviews conducted in the making of the documentary film *Stolen Babies of Spain* and this book by the same title.

300,000+- An estimate of the number of stolen baby victims directly violated, though victims place this at a much higher number.

600,000 to 1 million+- Estimated number of deaths during and just after the Spanish Civil War, this number includes executions ordered by Franco and those buried in unmarked or mass graves and ditches.

End Notes

PROLOGUE

1. Mafia- Though originally used as a term, similar to *La Cosa Nostra*, (Italian-"Our thing") to describe an organized and ruthless criminal network operating in Sicily and then expanded in a pejorative sense to describe a broad array of Italian and Italian-American criminal networks, victims in Spain use this term in a non-ethnic sense. They use this term to primarily describe a hidden, ruthless and powerful criminal network which operates with impunity and above the law. [see *The Mafia in Popular Culture*, history.com and *The History of the Mafia* by Salvatore Lupo (USA, 2009)].

2. The Second Republic of Spain (1931-1939)- A progressive period of Spanish politics and leadership which also triggered an ultra-conservative backlash, which aligned with the church in Spain helped form a military and political coalition led by Franco which seized power and ousted the legitimately elected Second Republic leaders. Under this Second Republic, a new Spanish Constitution was passed which in part, stripped Spanish nobility of any specialized legal status while guaranteeing freedom of speech and expression for all. The new constitution also took direct aim at weakening if not crippling the power of the Catholic Church in Spain (Preston 19).

Articles 26 and 27 barred religious orders coming from the ranks of educators, limited church education and their role in secular schools and placed strict controls and regulations on the church acquiring and expanding property and real estate holdings (Payne 632).

In part, Article 27 reads: "Freedom of conscience and the right to freely profess and practice any religion or no religion is

223

guaranteed in this, the Spanish territory." (Constitution of the Republic of Spain, Article 27, p. 11, scrbd.com), and further, "No one may be forced to officially declare their religious beliefs." (Constitution of the Republic of Spain, Article 27, p.11, scrbd.com). Under the leadership of Federica Montseny, the first woman minister in Spain (1936-1937), Spanish women achieved legal equality with men, gained the right to divorce and have abortions, as well as the right to vote. Laws were created to protect illegitimate children and legal prostitution was abolished. All this was codified under the Second Spanish Republic. (see also scrbd.com)

3. **Sister (*Sor*) María Gómez Valbuena** (1925-2013)- In addition to testimony and affidavits presented as part of the criminal case brought against her by the complainant Purificación Betegón, who accused Sor María of stealing her twin babies and selling them while deceiving her (Betegón) about her babies deaths, while she (Valbuena) worked at the Santa Cristina clinic in Madrid. *See also* a number of articles by *El País* leading up to and just after the indictment and death of Sor María (January of 2013).

4. **Antonio Vallejo-Nágera's Essays**- See his essays on positive eugenics and political purification in *Eugenesia de la Hispanidad y regeneración de la raza* (1937), and *Eugamia* (1938) a eugenic policy implemented through premarital orientation.

5. **Baby factory to the world**- According to many victims, this was simply a well-known fact, especially during the 1950s and 1960s under Franco. Francisco González de Tena, the noted Spanish sociologist and author whom we interviewed stressed this was known throughout and even informally marketed globally to attract tourists and consumers.

6. Falange- Prior to the Spanish Civil War, the Falange was an ultra-Nationalist and expansive political party led initially by the Spanish leader José Antonio Primo de Rivera. This Falange or "Phalanx" was later absorbed into the military dictatorship of Franco and shaped into a feared and ruthless, personal guard of Franco.

INTRODUCTION

1. Baby Stealing- While many identify the start of any organized baby stealing in Spain began in 1939, or just after the Spanish Civil War ended, the involuntary separation of mothers and their babies began even during the civil war hostilities in the so-called "Franco's Prisons." These were the prisons where Vallejo-Nágera did his "testing" and concluded that Republican women must be separated from their babies for the good of the nation and to begin the "purification" and elimination of the "red gene."

2. Former Supreme Court (Criminal Court) Judge Baltazar Garzón was the first who publicly placed the estimate of babies stolen in Spain. However, now many place the estimates much higher, including fraudulent and illegal adoptions. We often heard that 300,000 was now on the lower end of cases and those directly impacted.

CHAPTER 1

1. Nazi Eugenics and Nazi Eugenicists- Eugenics, as a social-psychological movement had already begun to flourish in the late 1800's and early 1900's (britannica.com/science/eugenics-genetics). At its base, Eugenics was, and remains, a belief, supposedly supported by science at the time, that modern society had a "moral imperative" (Bowler 309) to improve the lot of humanity by encouraging only "the ablest" (Bowler 309) people to reproduce and have offspring. German conservatives and Eugenicists, many aligned closely within the Nazi Party viewed the Weimar Republic and its overt liberalism as a "sick organism" www.alphahistory.com/nazigermany/nazi-eugenics) that had been allowed to "enter the bloodstream" of Germany and "contaminate" it (alphahistory.com/nazigermany/nazi-eugenics) and through strategic eugenics, "purify the race" of all "impure and weak elements" (alphahistory.com/nazigermany/nazi-eugenics) for a new, stronger Germany to rise again. Vallejo-Nágera actually began to investigate and research how Spain could transplant Nazi Eugenics to Spain under Franco as far back as post-World War I.

2. **Antonio Vallejo-Nágera's** more notable essays on his eugenics goals for Spain included; *Eugenesia de la Hispanidad* (1937) and *Eugamia* (1938), and lectures were on the subject of the need to apply the science of eugenic racism to "cleanse the Spanish race" of all the environmental factors that "incubated and nurtured" the unacceptable "Red Gene" of Marxism and the mental deficiencies of all the Republicans, especially the mothers and their offspring." (Preston *Spanish Holocaust* 514). Vallejo-Nágera made clear what he thought was at stake for Spain during the civil war, "Franco has been chosen by God to be the savior, the '*El Caudillo*' (Warlord) of Spain and to re-Christianize the land." (Richards *Morality and Biology* 42) Or, as he would also write, "To shout Franco is to shout 'God, Spain and Tradition'" (*Dios, España y Tradición*).

3. **Franco's Prisons**- Ironically, Antonio Vallejo-Nágera, who argued that Republican women were vile, disgusting and sub-human and based this on his field testing of them in these prisons, actually never directly interviewed any women, as he feared he would catch some infectious disease if he got close to any of them.

4. ***Putas, feas, rojas, peladas*** were typical insults hurled at Republican women or suspected sympathizers, *please see also Glossary Terms.*

5. *Señora* **Fidalgo's diary** tells of her experience as a young woman in Franco's Prisons. It goes into even more detail as to how she and others were treated by their captors and how the church supported their abuse.

6. Estimates of deaths vary, though numbers appear to keep increasing and more are being discovered as more mass graves are being identified in Spain, see also *The Spanish Holocaust Encyclopedia*.

7. An excellent work on **Vallejo-Nágera's role** in the acclimation and rise of Franco and his specific assertions is Spanish Holocaust (Preston).

8. Vallejo-Nágera often spoke of a **"red gene"** and Republican women as **"red gene carriers"** or simply **"red carriers"** (see Preston's *The Spanish Holocaust*, p. 514) and Vallejo-Nágera's essay *Eugnesia de la Hispanidad* (1937).

9. Walks of Shame used both to degrade and humiliate as well as the expulsion of any "communist demons" see Hernández, *Mujeres encarceladas la prisión de ventas. De la república al franquismo* 1931-1941 (2003).

10. The marrying of Franco and God and the Catholic Church has been well chronicled if not fully understood then or now, see as an example, Richards work in *Morality and Biology in the Civil War: Psychiatrists, Revolution and Women Prisoners in Malaga* (Contemporary European History 2001, p. 395-421).

11. A marker of deviant or red behavior often led to isolation and societal rejection or worse. For a good treatment of the psychology and strategy behind such marking, see Foucault, Michel and his work in discipline and punishment in *Discipline and Punish: The Birth of a Prison* (1995).

12. The December 1941 Adoption Law as well as a number of related reforms made it even easier and legal to take abandoned, involuntarily separated or even stolen babies and have them renamed and papers reworked to present far different portrait of ancestry and family relations.

13. ***Patronatos,*** **The** ***Patronato de Protección de la Mujer*** was a social services department for females created in 1941, directed by Franco's wife, Carmen Polo de Franco. These institutions were launched throughout Spain as a network aimed at policing women's behaviors and to closely watch their behavior in areas or events like movie cinemas, public swimming pools or dance venues that potentially could contravene the norms of the church regarding morality (Morcillo *En cuerpo y alma* 191). Part of this *Patronato* network of scrutiny included, organized street raids, encouraging and following up on complaints from relatives about immoral behavior. Often it took only one such complaint, even if unsubstantiated, to get a young girl now deemed "unruly" to be assigned to one of these *Patronato* care centers. Once assigned, voluntarily leaving the centers was almost impossible (Grosso 1). Once the female minors entered the centers, their parents lost legal custody, and the *Patronato* assumed all legal, custodial rights of the child.

14. **See in part** Vinyes, Ricard works on the ***Auxilios,*** including; *Irredentas. Las presas politicas y sus hijos en las cárceles franquistas* (2002) and Vinyes, Ricard Armengou, Montse et al., *Els nens perduts del franquisme* (2002).

15. ***Auxilio*** **or** ***Auxilio Social*** were facilities where children that were older than three years of age (abandoned, orphaned, displaced) and more difficult to place with loyal Nationalist families were then sent to these *Auxilio Social* institutions. They helped consolidate and mark Franco's domination over the vanquished. The psychologist Foucault explains that torture must "mark the victim and is intended, either by the scar it leaves on the body, or by the spectacle that accompanies it, to brand the victim with infamy" (*Discipline and Punish* 34). This is figuratively and literally what the State accomplished in these institutions, frequently torturing and abusing the children physically as well as mentally.

16. Sección Femenina de la Falange- Headed up by Pilar Primo de Rivera, the daughter of the former dictator of Spain, Miguel Primo de Rivera (1923-1930), and sister of José Antonio, the founder of the *Falange,* implemented the "fully body of disclosure) or *"Cuerpo de Divulgación,"* whose mission was to ensure that all eugenic policies under Franco were strictly enforced. This included no abortions, a mandate for women to be married prior to bearing children, and a broad promulgation for women to ensure that they "do not wittingly or unwittingly" have or pass on the "red gene" (Preston 515-516). Also see (mujeresycaridad.umwblogs.org).

17. See *Cuerpo de Divulgación* above.

18. Both marriage and happiness guides were created and distributed in 1953 and 1954 by the *Sección Femenina de la Falange* under the leadership of Pilar Primo de Rivera.

19. By close monitoring, scrutiny and use of sanctions, the *Sección Femenina* played a key role in isolating and further marking unwed, single women, essentially cutting off their options and opportunities.

20. See in part *Defensa de la Hispanidad* (Vallejo-Nágera and Maetzu), Preston (Spanish Holocaust) and for context prior, Llewellyn, Joseph (Nazi Eugenics).

21. *España es Diferente* really had a double-meaning, one focused on its diversity within the country aimed at western tourism (beaches, mountains, cosmopolitan cities, rural areas, desert) as well as a sense that it is different from its self-imposed period of political and global isolation under Franco.

22. Baby Factory- See Francisco González de Tena comments above.

23. Stolen baby victims point to evidence suggesting that the deniers of their issue are funded and encouraged by ultra-conservative factions who are the descendants of *Franquismo*.

CHAPTER 2

1. Many victims of whom never met each other or who were aware of each other's cases or stories, did share nearly verbatim quotes from nuns or nurses, doctors or priests who would tell them they are young and can have more babies or to simply love the children they still have after they were (falsely) told their babies had died.

2. We conducted over **300+ interviews** with victims and advocates between 2015 to early 2020. These interviews included those on and off-camera, in-person and in a few instances by phone. Throughout the book, the interviews shared, with the exception of the case files of Enrique Vila, have been transcribed and taken from these interviews exclusively in written form for this publication.

3. Journalists such as María José Esteso have written extensively on Dr, Vela and the allegations against him of using dead, frozen babies to deceive new mothers into thinking their baby had died. A French news reporter at one point filmed undercover a meeting with Dr. Vela where it appeared he admitted to doing such activities, or at the very least engaging in falsifying adoptions.

4. "We all Knew"- In our interview with former nun and Daughters of Charity member, Carmen del Mazo, she made it clear that the coordination and theft of babies was no accident.

CHAPTER 3

1. Archivado which literally means archived in English, refers to claims and cases brought forward by stolen baby victims which at the exclusive discretion of the *fiscal* or prosecutor is archived or filed away pending some change or additional evidence. Notably, the burden on investigation and accessing and collecting evidence is on the victim, not the state. Closed case means that the archived status essentially becomes permanent.

2. A False Son or Daughter or False Baby refers to the official papers associated with babies which shows each as the biological son or daughter of its adopted parents. This practice makes it even more difficult for stolen babies or illegally adopted babies to locate his or her true, biological parents years later as an adult. This is opposed to when adoptive parents clearly are identified on official papers as not being the biological parent(s) of their (adopted) baby.

3. The 2011 filing of a class action lawsuit by Enrique Vila and Antonio Barroso which consisted of over 200 separate claims or cases by stolen baby victims was then separated out or parceled out to regional and local *fiscalías* which many victims believe helped blunt the impact and power of this legal law suit.

4. Spina Bifida- The malformation of the spinal column at birth though relatively rare, does appear more often in females like Eva P., than males.

CHAPTER 4

1. Calumnia- As discussed in this book briefly, is not the same though it is similar to civil laws in the USA like slander (verbal) or libel (written) and even some elements of defamation of character or reputation. However, where evidence of speaking or writing the truth is seen as rebuttable to any claim of wrongdoing in the USA, in Spain, even with evidence on one's side, a jail term is possible if proper "accusation protocol" is not first followed.

2. We have reached out to the Minister of Defense of Spain (as of 2018) for comment to the claims made by Clara, though, to date (2020) we have not been responded to.

CHAPTER 5

1.   European Parliament Committee on Petitions, Chairwoman Jude Kirton-Darling (UK-MP) spoke with us in 2019 and shared her insight as to the frustrations of many of the victims due to the lack of follow-up by Spanish authorities with international recommendations and requests.

2.   Opus Dei formally, The Prelature of the Holy Cross and Opus Dei, is a powerful and influential institution within the Catholic Church with its prelates or leaders appointed by the Pope. It is also known for the fervor of its members, its strict orthodoxy, and has been portrayed as secretive, almost cult-like and obsessive with guarding the reputation of the church in both movies and fictional novels (see *The Da Vinci Code 2006* IMDB), *Da Vinci Code* (Novel, 2003, Dan Brown), *Opus Dei Unveiled* 2006, and *Opus Dei* 2016).

3.   Letters to the Pope (Enrique Vila)- Full title, first published in Italian in 2018 (*Lettere di un bastardo al Papa*) and in 2019 in Spanish (*Cartas de un bastardo al Papa*).

4. The law allowing all adopted children to access the records and names of their biological parents was first passed under the Aznar Administration in Spain.

CHAPTER 6

1. Foucault's theories include those on bio-power, gender suppression and the concept of being "marked" both physically and emotionally. This is nearly exclusively propagated upon the downtrodden, impoverished class and in Spain, children as well as Republican women or suspected sympathizers not loyal to Franco were marked in cruel, abusive, and humiliating fashion, at times, ending in death.

2. Several victims we interviewed shared similar experiences of their time in either the **Patronatos** or **Auxilios** as described in this chapter and in Chapter 1.

3. North Hollywood is located in the east San Fernando Valley Region of the city of Los Angeles in California. It has about 88,000 residents and has a large Hispanic population.

4. The Madrid Pact of 1953 was signed between the USA and Spain and was an effort to increase political, social and military cooperation between these nations and allowed for a military presence (military bases) of the US in Spain.

5. Interviews and testimonials shared with us in Chapter 6 regarding Sor María Gómez Valbuena are taken from both the case files of Enrique Vila, from our own interview transcripts (2015-2020), and from *El Mundo* article *"Los secretos de la gran ladrona de niños,"* (Arroyo 12/2013).

6. From *El Mundo* article *"Los secretos de la gran ladrona de niños,"* (Arroyo 12/2013).

7. Sister María Gómez Valbuena was indicted to face possible criminal prosecution stemming from allegations that she conspired and facilitated the theft of Purificación Betegón's twin babies, just days after she appeared in court her death was reported as well as news her body was immediately cremated.

CHAPTER 7

1. When we were told that filming was prohibited, even on an open street, we were filming the exterior of a Daughters of Charity convent where Sister María Gómez Valbuena had worked.

2. When we were accosted at a cemetery, we were at an open, public cemetery in Alicante, Spain.

3. Though cameras and any filming is prohibited in the inside of the *Valle de los Caídos* memorial, we observed in-person, several people taking pictures, filming and what appeared to be school children stepping on top of the gravestone of Francisco Franco. We were also struck that fresh flowers are placed on the gravestone of the former dictator Franco daily.

4. In 2018, the Spanish Parliament voted **"No Confidence"** in then Prime Minister Mariano Rajoy (Partido Popular) head of a conservative political party and ruling coalition, as a result he was succeeded by current Prime Minister Pedro Sánchez of the PSOE, a socialist political party.

5. Augusto Pinochet Ugarte (1915-2006) was the Chilean dictator who ousted the democratically elected president, Salvador Allende, in 1973 and was accused of a variety of human rights violations and crimes against humanity during his years in office.

CHAPTER 8

1. Guillermo Peña is becoming known as the stolen babies' lawyer for his voluminous legal representation of many victims with open cases and complaints.

2. Felipe González was the Prime Minister of Spain between 1982-1996 and was a member of the Socialist Workers Party (PSOE, *Partido Socialista Obrero Español*) which had publicly promised to be more supportive of stolen baby victims and those searching for family also lost during the civil war.

CHAPTER 9

1. *Guardia Civil* is a military force in Spain charged with police and civil control duties. It is under the formal control of the Minister of Defense and the Minister of the interior. It was founded in 1844 by Queen Isabel II, initially as a special force to protect royalty.

2. Dr. Vela actually never did return to open court. He argued he was too frail to return, a verdict was made in *abstentia*, and he died not long after the verdict.

CHAPTER 10

1. The estimates and figures used in this chapter describing the epidemic of baby and children kidnapping and trafficking as well as outright selling was taken off of the most recent United Nations reports on these issues as well as from the International

Labor Organization's (ILO) annual report on forced child labor in conjunction with child trafficking.

2. One of the more noteworthy and underreported fact is the role of the USA historically, as the main consumer in terms of sheer numbers of illegal or improper baby adoptions and trafficking as well as domestic (USA) baby stealing and selling. The Tann case in Tennessee is but the most well-known but far from the only case. (*Beulah George "Georgia" Tann, 1891-1950, main area of operations was Memphis, TN*).

3. Domestic Spain DNA Labs- It continues to be a strongly held sentiment among victims in Spain that domestic Spanish labs, some of which are either owned and/or operated privately by Opus Dei, are not trustworthy. As a result, more and more victims are turning to USA based DNA testing and matching labs like *23andMe*, *MyHeritage* or *Ancestry*. The problem is that many of those whom the victims seek are not in those databases yet.

4. The Irish Examiner and AP News have followed this story, domestically and internationally. See in particular, Winfield, Nicole and de Cristofaro, Pietro, *Pope apologizes for crimes against Irish women and babies* (Aug. 26, 2018).

Author Profiles

Greg Rabidoux is an award-winning documentary film director (*Stolen Babies of Spain*) and the co-author of *Stolen Babies of Spain: The Book* as well as author of *Hollywood Politicos, Then and Now* (2008), and theatrical plays including; *Red Scared* and *The Diva*. Greg has also appeared as an actor in film, including *Death at Dinner*. He is co-founder of ValMar Productions Inc., and ValMar Films. He has an earned PhD, specializing in politics and film and a law degree from Marquette University Law school. Currently, he is directing pre-production for the upcoming documentary film *Stolen Babies of Serbia*.

Maravillas (Mara) Lencina is executive producer of the award-winning documentary film, *Stolen Babies of Spain* and co-author of *Stolen Babies of Spain: The Book*. Mara is a native of Alicante, Spain. Mara has conducted over 300 interviews with victims both for the film and her doctoral dissertation (*Giving Voice to the Voiceless: Testimonies of Stolen Baby Victims during the Franco Dictatorship*). Mara' s PhD is from Florida State University and she teaches Spanish at HGTC in South Carolina. She is co-founder of ValMar Productions Inc., and ValMar Films. Mara is a former professional tennis player on the WTA tour.

Enrique Vila Torres is a well-known advocate and lawyer for stolen baby victims specializing in facilitating encounters or reunions of separated family members. He has argued cases internationally, including before the United Nations, is a frequent expert guest on Spanish television and a prolific author on this subject, including; *Lettere Di Un Bastardo Al Papa* (2018), *Hijos de Otros Dioses* (2013) and *Bastardos* (2010). Enrique is also a victim and continues his own personal search for his biological mother. He lives in Spain with his family.

For more information about the stolen babies of Spain victims and their search for truth, justice and reconciliation or to learn how you can help, please visit the following website: www.stolenbabiesofspain.com

To learn about the award-winning documentary film Stolen Babies of Spain, please visit:
www.stolenbabiesofspain.com
www.facebook.com/stolenbabiesofspain
www.imdb.com/title/tt11219178/

Made in the USA
Las Vegas, NV
27 September 2022

56085377R00136